Mommy RESCUE Guide

Toddler Meals

S0-AFN-910

Lifesaving Recipes and Advice for Making Fun, Nutritious Food

Shana Priwer and Cynthia Phillips

Adams Media
Avon, Massachusetts

Copyright © 2007 by F+W Publications, Inc.
All rights reserved.
Contains material adopted and abridged from *The Everything®
Cooking for Baby and Toddler Book*, by Shana Priwer and Cynthia
Phillips, Copyright © 2006 by F+W Publications, Inc., and *The
Everything® Toddler Book*, by Linda Sonna, Ph.D., Copyright ©
2002 by F+W Publications, Inc.

Published by Adams Media, an F+W Publications Company
57 Littlefield Street
Avon, MA 02322
www.adamsmedia.com

ISBN 10: 1-59869-331-X
ISBN 13: 978-1-59869-331-7

Printed in China.
J I H G F E D C B A

Library of Congress Cataloging-in-Publication Data
available from the publisher

This publication is designed to provide accurate and authoritative
information with regard to the subject matter covered. It is sold
with the understanding that the publisher is not engaged in render-
ing legal, accounting, or other professional advice. If legal advice
or other expert assistance is required, the services of a competent
professional person should be sought.
—From a *Declaration of Principles* jointly adopted by a
Committee of the American Bar Association and
a Committee of Publishers and Associations

Many of the designations used by manufacturers and sellers to
distinguish their product are claimed as trademarks. Where those
designations appear in this book and Adams Media was aware of
a trademark claim, the designations have been printed with initial
capital letters.

*This book is available at quantity discounts for bulk purchases.
For information, please call 1-800-289-0963.*

Mommy Rescue Guide

Welcome to the lifesaving *Mommy Rescue Guide* series! Each *Mommy Rescue Guide* offers techniques and advice written by recognized parenting authorities.

These engaging, informative books give you the help you need when you need it the most! The *Mommy Rescue Guides* are quick, issue-specific, and easy to carry anywhere and everywhere.

You can read one from cover to cover or just pick out the information you need for rapid relief! Whether you're in a bind or you have some time, these books will make being a mom painless and fun!

Being a good mom has never been easier!

Contents

Introduction

EVERY MOMMY SHOULD MEET her recommended daily allowance of *Mommy Rescue Guide: Toddler Meals*! Whether your baby can say the words "Mommy, what's for dinner" or not, every mother knows that something nutritious should be her answer to the toddler mealtime dilemma. But it's not always easy to provide healthy food your child will actually eat!

In this book, you will find two chapters that discuss the importance of smart food choices, the reasons to go all-the-way homemade, and persuasion techniques appropriate for different stages of your toddler's growth.

Then you will find 200 recipes that will tempt your toddler's taste buds—and test the waters a bit. Split into chapters by stages of toddlerhood, each recipe section contains both basic and bold recipes for your growing toddler. From the time that you first introduce solid foods, try the Steamy Zucchini, until your two year old sits at the dinner table and chows down on a *special toddler* version of your Shepard's Pie, these recipes will make you both smile!

With strategies and recipes based on real-life successes and fiascos, this book contains foolproof advice on how to make mealtime fun, introduce new taste sensations, and treat your toddler to the wide world of food. Enjoy this time with your child—for mealtime is a time for experimenting, learning, and growing together!

Part 1

Introduction to Feeding Your Toddler

Chapter 1

Is My Toddler Normal?

BABIES REACH A NUMBER of important milestones in their first year. And you're probably watching out for them everyday. Smiling, giggling, sitting up, crawling, walking, and taking that first mouthful of solid food are achievements that contribute to your baby's growing independence. New parents are especially infatuated with their baby's first foods because, after all, eating is fun! We love to eat, and so do our children. Creating and consuming meals that both nourish and please is highly satisfying for all involved.

Appetite, Too Big, Too Small, Just Right

As you watch your baby grow, you may be amazed at how quickly her little body and mind develop. In fact, during the first twelve months of life, children triple their birth weight, gaining about 1 to 2 pounds per month. But things start to slow down between twelve and twenty-four months, when toddlers typically gain only 4 to 6 pounds—less than ½ pound per month. Between twenty-four and thirty-six months, they only gain 3½ to 5½ pounds—just over ⅓ pound per month! And those are averages, so some months they'll gain even less!

Since the beginning of the toddler years is also when parents try to get them to eat a greater variety of foods, it is easy to assume that resistance is due to being finicky. But consider the following:

- When toddlers consume very little food, it's probably because they just aren't hungry or haven't become accustomed to a new flavor!
- Unless your child's pediatrician suggests a need to spur weight gain, don't focus on how much a child is eating, but rather ensure that the quality of the little food consumed is excellent.
- If your child is losing weight or you're concerned about an overly dainty appetite, discuss the matter with your pediatrician.

Wean on Me

Breastfeeding has allowed your baby to turn into the strong toddler that he is today. But it is unusual to see toddlers nursing, because most parents struggle in earnest to wean them from the bottle or breast early in the second year of life. It is interesting to consider that in societies where nature is allowed to take its course, self-weaning occurs between ages 3 and 4; the minimum age is 2½. When they are ready to stop nursing, children simply taper off and lose interest. Whenever you choose to wean is fine, just realize that you will need to provide your toddler with the appropriate foods to keep his development on track.

If you try to wean a toddler before he's ready, it will most likely be difficult. Remember that weaning seems like severing a powerful emotional attachment—but there are things that you can do to soften the blow. Try some of the following:

- Choose a time when the youngster isn't coping with other major stresses.
- Tell your child you are going to wean him.
- Provide milk in a cup with meals.
- Nurse after meals, when the child has less of an appetite.
- Eliminate one bottle or nursing session at a time, beginning with the one the child is least attached to—typically in the middle of the day.
- Avoid the cues that trigger the desire to be nursed by staying busy and sitting in a different chair.

Smart Mommy

The American Association of Pediatrics recommends that breastfeeding continue for at least twelve months, and "thereafter for as long as mutually desired." The World Health Organization recommends "two years of age or beyond." And weaning at eighteen months is even associated with higher IQ!

- Spend the time you would have devoted to nursing reading a story, reciting nursery rhymes, or playing together.
- Offer bottle-fed babies a bottle of water.
- Wait five days before eliminating a second bottle or nursing session.
- Eliminate bedtime feedings last. (Provide other kinds of comfort until the child learns to fall asleep without being nursed. If possible, have Dad handle bedtime.)

Baby Meet Solid . . . Solid, Baby

If you are still nursing a one-year-old you should keep in mind that breastmilk alone does not meet his nutritional requirements. If you plan on breast-feeding exclusively past six months, consult your pediatrician for information on how to supplement your baby's diet.

As a rule of thumb, once your baby is a toddler, he needs solid food! At first, your tot may be reluctant but if you introduce new foods gradually, at least two to three days apart, he will get used to the new tastes and textures. Also, it is important to watch out for food allergies during this time. Common symptoms of food allergy include itchy, watery eyes, repeated sneezing attacks, itchy skin, clear mucus running from the nose, rash, hives, very red cheeks, or behavioral changes.

Five Meals a Day?

Because toddler tummies are still small, offer them five small meals a day rather than three big ones. An easy way to keep youngsters nutritionally well primed is to serve between-meal snacks that emphasize finger foods. That way, toddlers can more readily manage the mechanics of eating themselves, and there's less cooking and cleanup for the chef. (Remember not to let them wander as they munch!)

Popular Finger Foods
- Cheese sandwiches (cut in quarters)
- Hard-boiled egg slices
- Luncheon meat in a pita
- Fish-shaped crackers
- Mozzarella cheese sticks
- Fortified cereal
- Vegetable sticks
- Fruit wedges
- Whole-wheat crackers

From Table to Tummy

For a decade, parents were told to let youngsters decide what to eat. Adults were instructed to put the food on the table, and then sit back, relax, and let nature take its course. According to a widely publicized study, when little ones were offered a selection of nutritious foods and allowed to eat whatever they wished without parental interference—although they might fill up on potatoes for a meal or two—over the course of a week they consumed a diet that would make a nutritionist smile. The media urged parents to stop worrying and back off, reassuring them that if tots were allowed to follow their instincts, they would consume what their bodies needed.

As you may have guessed, there was a catch, but few reporters bothered to mention it: Everything that the scientists placed before their little research subjects was a healthy choice. Coca-Cola and M&Ms were not on the menu! If you want to trust Mother Nature to guide your toddler in the right direction, every dish you serve would have to be something She made herself. And that wise woman of the cosmos doesn't bake Ding Dongs, stir up batches of Jell-O Pudding, or make trips to McDonald's!

Little Tummies

Theories about food and methods of feeding are constantly changing. You may remember, as most American adults do, being pushed to "clean your plate" and to "eat more!" The result has been an

Mommy Must
Always be aware of your child's weight, not just as a baby, but as they grow throughout their childhood.

epidemic of weight problems. Ask yourself this question: are you saying those same things to your child? Even parents who don't use heavy-handed tactics to pass on their poor eating habits routinely provide not-so-subtle nudges, crooning, "This broccoli is so delicious," hoping their youngster will get the hint and eat, never mind that he's not hungry. Your child's stomach needs tell him when he is full. Don't teach him to listen to you instead of to his own body!

What about all that mashing and banging and tossing and rolling to experience food in all its most disgusting forms? Pediatrician and bestselling author T. Berry Brazelton believes that allowing toddlers to linger and play with their food in hopes a random bite will end up in their tummies should be a no-no, too. There are less messy ways, he contends, for kids to enhance their motor skills.

Alarmed by the appalling height/weight statistics (a majority are now decidedly overweight), the rise in kiddie cholesterol, the obsession with dieting (one-third of nine-year-old girls claim they're trying to shed pounds), and the exponential growth of eating disorders among teens and young adults, Dr. Brazelton presents a minimum daily diet in his book, *Touchpoints: The Essential Reference*:

- 16 ounces of milk (or the equivalent in cheese, yogurt, or ice cream)
- 2 ounces of protein or complex carbohydrates high in iron (meat, an egg, or fortified cereal)
- 1 ounce of orange juice or fresh fruit

- 1 multivitamin (but only if absolutely necessary to eliminate the vegetable wars)

Of course, toddlers shouldn't be allowed to supplement this fare with foods that are essentially nutrition-free! If this meager menu isn't sufficient, offer them healthy food choices.

Why Homemade?

Are you tempted to stock up on baby cereal and quick-fix snacks for you toddler? While a stocked pantry is not a bad idea, this book is about homemade food! You may ask yourself: Why should I make my own baby food when so much is pre-made for me, sold in supermarkets, and is ready to go? For starters, try convenience! Pre-made rice cereal must be mixed with water, breastmilk, or formula, and can't be stored once you've mixed it. Store-bought baby foods are often several servings' worth for young babies, and can't be stored if you feed directly out of the jar.

Those cute little jars of baby food you see on the supermarket shelves will also leave a not-so-cute dent

Mindful Mommy
In the case of juice, more is not better! It can cause rapid tooth decay because of its high sugar content. It's important that it be fed only in a cup and that a regular toothbrushing routine be established. Juice can also cause digestive problems. Try offering your tot water occasionally instead!

in your wallet. Jarred baby food is more expensive than homemade, particularly for large inexpensive vegetables such as sweet potatoes. For the price of a single large sweet potato (which might make 4–8 jars worth), you could purchase only 1–2 jars of the pre-made version. Doing it yourself will save money almost every time.

And don't forget about taste. Store-bought foods often taste like they've been sitting around for a while, and their flavors are flat. Babies know the difference! Nutrition is also a concern. While single-ingredient jarred baby foods are made without preservatives or spices, most fresh fruits and vegetables will lose some of their vitamins during the jarring process. Fresh home-made purées are the best thing you can feed young babies because they retain the vitamins and minerals.

Finally, you know what's in the food that you pre-pare. You never have to worry about salt, sugar, or any mysterious ingredients that might go into your child's delicate stomach. You have control over what you feed your baby when making your own food, and you can tailor your recipes to baby's developing preferences.

What to Offer First

Okay, so you're beginning to see that homemade, home-cooked, healthy foods are the way to go. But how do you get started? Typically, the first foods include cereals, single fruits, and single vegetables. It's important to wait a few days between new foods;

you'll want to make sure baby does not develop any sort of allergic reaction before offering more foods that are new. Cereals are the least likely to spark an allergic reaction, so they're usually a safe first food.

Allergic reactions can be very scary, but sometimes there are ways to avoid them. In your child's first couple of years, there are certain foods you should just stay away from. For example, be sure to avoid anything with wheat and eggs for the first 6 months, as both are common allergens. Avoid egg whites until an infant is 1 year old. Honey should also be avoided until baby is at least a year old, because it can contain a dangerous botulism spore. If your family has any history of allergy to nuts, avoid peanuts or any products with tree nuts until your child is at least three years old. Without a family history of peanut or tree nut allergies, it's relatively safe to introduce nut butters from about 12 months on. Experts usually recommend that parents avoid nuts and other "allergic" foods if their baby has any of these risk factors:

1. The infant already has an allergy to another food.
2. The infant has other "allergic" type disorders, such as eczema, asthma, or hay fever.
3. The infant has family members with food allergies, eczema, allergies, or asthma.

Remember that the goal of feeding in the first year is mostly about getting baby used to different tastes and textures. Breastmilk or formula will still provide most of the calories and other nutrients to baby's diet through the first year.

Utensils You'll Need

It's just mashed up solid food, right? Well, not exactly. While some baby foods can be made with nothing more than the silverware you already have, others require more in the way of equipment. Very ripe fruits, such as avocados, bananas, and pears can be mashed with a fork. That's it! They don't require cooking or puréeing.

For the meat-and-vegetable purées, or any of the more complex recipes for younger babies, you'll need more than a fork. Consider purchasing a food processor, blender, food mill, "mini" chopper, or other machine that will grind and pulse your food into a purée. These tools range dramatically in price and capacity, so choose accordingly based on your needs. Do you plan to make only enough food for one or two servings at a time? If so, go with a smaller model. If you want to make a month's worth, consider a full-sized food processor.

Mindful Mommy

New supplies can be fun and very useful. You can finally break out all those cute baby bibs you received as shower gifts! Plastic placemats strategically placed around the room will catch the leaks or you could purchase a large splat mat to put under the highchair. Even enlist the family pet to pitch in with clean-up!

Thicker purées usually can be thinned with water but, even so, some may have too grainy a texture. Use a food strainer (or even a pasta strainer) to further thin your purées before serving. Another very useful tool is a mortar and pestle—rice, oats, and other grains can be ground to a powder quickly and easily, especially for small amounts.

When it comes time to feed your baby, consider using coated spoons. These are small baby-sized spoons that have plastic or rubber tips. They're available in stores, inexpensive, and perfect for baby's sensitive mouth. Many of these spoons are heat-sensitive, and will quickly change colors to warn you if the food you're about to serve is too hot.

Storage Concerns

What if you get carried away one Sunday afternoon and you have baby food for a week? What do you do then? Well, there are many safe ways to store home-made baby food. Some families stock up on freezer-safe glass jars and lids, and freeze a container's worth at a time. This technique works well, as long as you

Smart Mommy
Label everything you put in the freezer to avoid surprises!

remember to let the food cool before freezing. Also, don't fill the jars up to the rim because the food will expand as it freezes. Plastic freezer containers will also work, but look for smaller containers. You can recycle commercial baby food jars for freezing, but because they weren't designed to be frozen, they may explode in the freezer. Freezer-safe glass or plastic is the best for this storage.

Another popular technique is to freeze baby food in ice cube trays. This allows for single-serving storage, which is a great idea for babies who don't consume very much at one sitting. Look for ice cube trays with covers; if unavailable, wrap the ice cube tray in plastic wrap before storing. Once the food is frozen, you can tip out the baby food cubes into a plastic freezer bag, remove, and thaw one cube at a time.

Always label your baby food with the ingredients and date of storage.

Most homemade baby foods will keep in the freezer for about three months, so be sure to rotate through your older stock as you add new meals to the freezer. Once you've thawed a container of baby food and are storing it in the refrigerator, use it within a day or two.

Generally, baby food is safe to serve if it has freezer burn. Freezer burn results when extra air gets into the food. It is different from the ice crystals that often appear on baby food. These crystals result from all the liquid in most baby foods. The icy or frozen part of the food will taste drier than the rest, but it can be removed before heating.

Frozen baby food can be thawed in any number of ways. Most foods will thaw in the refrigerator within about four hours, and this is one of the safer methods. Never leave baby food out on the counter to thaw, especially if it contains meat, because it may gather bacteria and become unsafe. Baby food can be thawed in a saucepan on the stove, or in the microwave, but stir frequently, and be sure to test the temperature before serving. Once you've thawed a container of baby food, don't refreeze it unless you've cooked it first.

Don't Get Carried Away

A word of caution: even though your food processor is your favorite new toy, there are some things that you should avoid! Once you've gotten the hang of making baby food, it may be tempting to start puréeing everything in sight. And, once your baby is about one year old, you can serve her most of the same foods that you would consume. However, there are a few items that you should either wait on, or purchase pre-made.

Root vegetables (carrots, beets, turnips) and leafy green vegetables (spinach, lettuce, collard greens) can contain more nitrates than most other vegetables. This is mostly because these vegetables have more exposure to soil and ground water. Excess nitrates in young babies can lead to problems with your child's oxygen saturation, a rare but potentially fatal problem. Because of the high concentration of nitrates in these vegetables, it's best to wait either until your baby is seven or eight months old, or use commercially prepared versions if you want to feed them to your baby. Commercial baby food manufacturers can screen for nitrate levels in their vegetables, but this screening can't be done at home. If you choose to make your own versions of these foods earlier than eight months, avoid using the cooking water as a liquid thinner (since it will contain additional nitrates) and use organic vegetables, which aren't grown in nitrate fertilizer.

Once your toddler starts eating "chewing foods," or ones that require a few more teeth, you will also need to be very aware of choking hazards. Foods such as hot dogs, grapes, peanuts, and popcorn are dangerous for children who do not yet chew their food thoroughly, and these should be avoided altogether or fed to a child only under close supervision.

Mommy Must

Babies take a long time to experience food. They savor new flavors and often love new textures. Because babies explore the world through sensory play, don't be surprised if sweet potatoes soon become hair gel! It's a messy process but a necessary one. Your baby is learning an important new skill, how to eat!

Texture Trouble

The new textures of solid food will amaze babies. Their mouths will experience new sensations with each bite! So you may be wondering: how creamy does her food need to be? While most six-month-olds are still content to eat food that has been 100 percent puréed, some (especially early teethers) will be ready for more textured food. Around six or seven months, try offering foods that haven't been puréed into submission; pulse the food processor enough to grind up the meal, but leave it slightly coarser. Experiment with what your baby will tolerate. If your baby closes her mouth or appears to gag on every bite, go back to the smoother foods for a few days.

Gradually start introducing more discrete bites of food. Biter biscuits, teething crackers, and other meltaway-style foods will help your baby gain confidence and also help her get used to swallowing food with texture. She'll eventually get used to the "Stage 3"-style meals that you prepare for her, which will include purées mixed with some lumpier textures.

Some babies even jump straight to the real thing! If your child expresses no interest in lumpier textures, try offering small bites of the genuine article. Sweet potatoes can be fork-mashed and picked up by little fingers, and some babies will prefer self-feeding at a very early age. Look to your child for cues as to how to prepare her meals.

Un-Fancy Dining

Stay away from processed foods! Simple, natural, and healthy foods are the name of the game. Use this time with your baby to teach her how to eat well—that means balanced, nutritious, untreated foods. You're lucky, the world of food is brand-new to your baby, and she's easily impressed by the simplest of choices. Fruits and vegetables are naturally sweet, and baby food never requires salt, sugar, or other spices. Avoid pre-made cookies, crackers, or other snacks that contain these unnecessary ingredients. There's no reason to give your baby an artificial sweet tooth!

It's also a good idea to skip the bacon and sausage. Babies don't need processed foods, which are difficult to digest and may cause upset stomachs. Stick to simple and natural foods, avoiding anything greasy or full of spice. In other words, feed your baby the way that you should feed yourself!

Some parents, seeing their baby's chubby cheeks and thighs, feed their babies low- or even nonfat yogurt. This is a mistake. Lower-fat dairy products should not be given until your child is at least two years old (and nonfat products should be avoided

Mommy Knows Best

Just as there are foods that keep people awake, there are foods that promote sleep in babies. A snack that combines a food high in tryptophan with a complex carbohydrate can help induce feelings of well-being and slow brain activity. Try feeding your little one pieces of turkey, pasta, cheese, chicken, and rice.

until your child is closer to 5 years old). Fat is necessary for proper brain development, and the extra calories are necessary to supplement baby's diet. The American Academy of Pediatrics recommends that babies get approximately half their calories from fat; this amount decreases to $\frac{1}{3}$ of their daily requirement after they reach 2 years of age. It is therefore a good idea to feed your baby whole milk after one year, if a mother is no longer breastfeeding, and try whole-fat yogurt and cheese after nine months.

Setting out to prepare your baby's food from fresh, organic produce is a wonderful ambition. You'll rest assured that your baby is getting the most nutritious food she could possibly have. Don't get discouraged, though, if you end up substituting. Not all vegetables are available year-round. Take advantage of what's seasonally available, exercise care in food preparation and storage, and be proud of your accomplishment!

Chapter 2

What Does My Toddler Need?

FILLING A TODDLER TUMMY with food is easy. Filling it with nutritious foods to meet the needs of a growing dynamo, and instilling healthy habits that last a lifetime can pose major challenges. This is a prime time for power struggles—avoid begging, bribing, pressuring, and punishing to get youngsters to open up and swallow. The fact is, toddlers actually need very few calories.

Open Wide, It's Good for You

Eating a healthy and balanced diet is tough for everyone! It's no different for your baby. When it comes to menu planning, variety is important for more than making toddler taste buds tingle. No single food is perfect, so children need to eat many different foods for optimal nutrition. For instance, oranges are rich in vitamin C but lack vitamin B12. Apricots are high in beta-carotene. Scientists have only just begun to unravel the exact components of plants and animals that are good for humankind, and they continue to add to the list.

Only a few generalities are certain: fresh foods are better than processed; pesticide-free food is healthier. So take up cooking and go organic! The typical American diet consists of so much poor-quality food. In order to know what your baby is eating, take the time to look at all of the food labels!

Sources of Calories

Source	Amount	Approximate Number of of Calories
Protein	1 gram	4
Carbohydrate	1 gram	4
Fat	1 gram	9

The first thing chefs need to know is that besides supplying vitamins, minerals, and other ingredients needed for good health (such as fiber), foods provide energy. Energy is measured in calories. Calories, which are measured in grams, come from three sources: proteins, fats, and sugars. Children need all three. Parents need to keep track of which kind of calories their youngsters consume to be sure they are getting enough of each.

The number of calories needed depends on a toddler's individual metabolism, growth rate, and activity level, so the average number of calories a child needs at any particular time will vary. Large, active toddlers need more calories; small, sedentary toddlers need fewer. Foods that are low in fat can still be high in calories if they contain a lot of sugar. You must read the labels to determine how many calories a food actually contains. Here are some general guidelines:

Recommended Daily Calories

Age	1	2	3
Protein (15%)	165	180	195
Carbohydrates (55%)	605	660	715
Fat (30%)	330	360	390
Total (100%)	1,100	1,200	1,300

Nutritional Pyramid, Road Map to Healthy Eating

Everyone can learn a thing or to from the Nutritional Pyramid. You might think that what you are eating is healthy, or at least healthy enough. But take another look; you might be surprised at what you see! What started as the Four Food Groups is now the Nutritional Pyramid. The following sections provide details on specific serving sizes, but the pyramid is a handy visual reference. The habits formed now will help keep your child healthy as he grows.

Protein Counts

As you may know, protein is important for a healthy diet. And it is important for children and adults equally. Protein can be found in meats,

poultry, fish, eggs, nuts, and beans. It's the extras—
the skin and fat or addition of oil for frying, butter
for baking, and cream sauces for smothering—that
quickly add to the calories from fat. Milk, cheese,

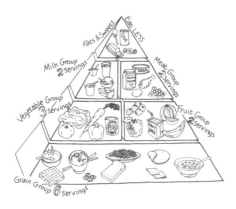

and yogurt are also high in protein and are rich
sources of another essential nutrient, calcium. Low-
fat products are preferable for children over age two
because they have fewer calories from fat. Provide
two to four toddler servings of meat and high-protein
alternatives daily, and three to four servings of milk,
yogurt, and cheese. One toddler serving equals:

- 1 whole egg or 2 whites
- ¼ cup baked beans
- ¾ cup milk
- 3 slices turkey luncheon meat
- ¼ cup nonfat dry milk
- ¾ ounce hard cheese

- ½ cup yogurt
- ¾ ounce poultry, meat, or fish
- 3 tablespoons cottage cheese
- 1½ tablespoons peanut butter

Servings of Complex Carbohydrates

Bread, rice, cereal, and pasta, are made primarily or wholly from grains. All of these foods contain complex carbohydrates—you've probably heard about these. Complex carbohydrates provide energy. Toddlers should eat six to eleven servings per day. To help you figure out what you are feeding your toddler, look at the following chart. One toddler serving equals:

- ½ slice whole-grain bread
- ⅓ cup cold cereal
- ¼ English muffin
- ¼ cup cooked pasta or rice (brown or wild is best)
- ¼ whole-grain bagel
- 2 to 3 whole-wheat crackers
- ¼ cup hot cereal

Mindful Mommy
Contrary to what many people think, grains are healthy foods and are not fattening. It's when you add butter, cheese, whole milk, and assorted fat-rich sauces that the calories from fat quickly add up.

Keep the Fat

As adults in America we are conditioned to avoid fat at all costs. When your child gets older, you should be aware of how much fat she is eating, especially after age two—processed foods tend to be loaded with fat. But when it comes to your baby or toddler, don't worry too much about round tummies and folds. Toddlers don't need low-fat diets unless there's a special reason! Parents should provide five to eight servings per day from ages twelve to twenty-four months, and add a half serving to each end of the range from ages twenty-four to thirty-six months.

One toddler serving equals:

- ¾ cup whole milk or yogurt
- 9 French fries
- 1½ cups 2 percent milk
- 2 chicken nuggets
- 1 tablespoon peanut butter
- 1½ ounces beef, lamb, or pork
- 1 egg
- ½ tablespoon oil, butter, margarine, or mayonnaise
- 2½ ounces poultry
- ½ cup ice cream

The World Health Organization has recommended adding DHA (docosahexaenoic acid), a fatty acid found in mother's milk, to formula for bottle-fed tots. Studies show it can make a significant difference in mental and physical development. European formula manufacturers now include it in their recipes. Check with your pediatrician.

Eat Veggies

Start off on the right foot—introduce veggies at a young age and your little one will be used to eating them on a daily basis. Vegetables are great because they contain small amounts of protein. What makes vegetables so important are the vitamins and fiber they also contain. Most of the vitamins are lost in the canning process. The recommended daily allowance (RDA) charts on packaged foods list how much of needed vitamins and other nutrients foods contain. If you're using a lot of preprocessed foods, learn to read the labels! Keep these points in mind:

1. Frozen vegetables are better than canned since fewer vitamins are lost in processing. Vegetables lightly steamed in cookware with a tight-fitting lid are better still. Raw vegetables are best of all.
2. Starchy vegetables like potatoes and yams are especially rich in nutrients, but they become a less-than-great choice when fat—butter, cheese, gravy, sour cream, or oil—is added.
3. Beans, which are rich in vitamins and fiber as well as protein, can meet vegetable or protein requirements.

Fruit Dude (or Dudette)

Fruit should be an easy sell. It is naturally sweet and fun to mush around in your baby's hands. Fruit—

including fresh, dried, frozen, and home-squeezed into juice—is also rich in vitamins, especially vitamin C. Beware of fruit canned in sugary syrup, and juices that contain mostly sugar and only a squirt of real fruit juice.

A few drops can result in a label that proclaims in large letters, "Contains real juice!" The question is how much juice, and you must read the label to find out.

Offer two or more servings of fruit per day. One serving equals approximately 1 tablespoon per year of life, so two-year-olds need at least 4 tablespoons per day. The equivalent is:

- ½ cup (4 ounces) of juice
- 3 to 4 tablespoons of fruit

And Don't Forget . . .

So that's it right? Just find a balance of the things listed above and you're good to go? No! There are some key things that everyone needs, that may be a little bit more difficult to find. It is important for everyone—you and your baby—to include fiber, calcium, liquids, vitamins, and minerals into their diet.

Think Fiber

Fiber is important for proper functioning of the bowels. Hefty portions serve as an antidote for chronic constipation. Offer three or more servings of vegetables per day. One serving equals approximately

1 tablespoon per year of life, so two-year-olds need at least 6 tablespoons per day. Besides raw vegetables, other high-fiber foods include whole-grain breads and cereals, beans and peas, and fruit.

Bones Count on Calcium

Calcium is required for bone growth, so to ensure your child gets enough calcium, you will need to provide daily doses from another source. Good choices include broccoli, calcium-fortified orange juice, calcium-fortified soymilk, canned sardines or salmon (with the bones), goat's milk, kale, tofu, and turnip greens.

Lots of Liquids

Liquids are important for everyone. You should give your toddler 4 to 6 cups of liquids daily under normal circumstances—more in hot weather or if they are ill with fever, vomiting, or diarrhea. Besides water (from the tap or bottled, plain or carbonated), good sources of liquids include soup, fruit or vegetable juices, and milk.

But note that milk provides only $\frac{2}{3}$ cup of liquid per cup served; the rest is solids. Also, many bottled waters do not contain fluoride. Either choose a brand

Smart Mommy

Children need lots of iron to grow tall and strong. There are many iron-rich foods that you can give your child, including beef, liver, dried peas and beans, dried fruit, blackstrap molasses, and wheat germ. Also, one of the best sources is iron-fortified cereal. To help with iron absorption, serve food rich in vitamin C at the same meal.

and get the chemical composition from the bottler, or have your child drink tap water instead.

Recommended Daily Allowances (RDAs)

The RDAs for children ages one through three are as follows (according to *Smart Medicine for a Healthier Child* by Janet Zand, Rachel Walton, and Bob Rountree):

RDAs

Substance	Recommended Daily Amount
Protein	16 g (grams)
Vitamin A	400 mcg (micrograms)
Vitamin D	10 mcg
Vitamin E	6 mg (milligrams)
Vitamin K	15 mcg
Vitamin B1	0.7 mg
Vitamin B2	0.8 mg
Vitamin B3	9 mg
Vitamin B5	3 mg
Vitamin B6	1 mg
Vitamin B12	0.7 mcg
Vitamin C	40 mg
Biotin	20 mcg
Folic Acid	50 mcg
Calcium	800 mg
Magnesium	80 mg
Phosphorus	800 mg
Potassium	1,000 mg (age 1–2), 1,400 mg (age 2–3)
Sodium	225 mg (age 1–2), 300 mg (age 2–3)
Chromium	20–80 mcg
Copper	0.7 mg
Iron	10 mg
Selenium	20 mcg
Zinc	10 mg
Iodine	70 mcg
Fluoride	0.7 mg

Good Vitamins

Vitamins don't have to come in the form of a pill. Many foods are rich in vitamins, so it's easy to include these in your child's diet. Specifically, it's important to include at least one vitamin A–rich and one vitamin C–rich food in children's diets each day.

Foods rich in vitamin A include: apricots, broccoli, Brussels sprouts, cantaloupe, carrots, green leafy vegetables, mangos, papayas, and sweet potatoes.
Foods rich in vitamin C include: bell peppers, broccoli, cantaloupe, citrus, kiwi, mangos, papayas, peaches, potatoes (with skin), strawberries, sweet potatoes, and tomatoes.

As you can see, there are several foods that supply both vitamins.

Special Bodies, Special Needs

Playing chef can be really fun! There is something very special about being able to cook something special for someone you love. Since every child is different, becoming their personal chef will allow you to cater your child's special needs.

The nutritional requirements of every child are different. Some children's bodies are unable to absorb proper amounts of iron, so they need a supplement. Also, many toddlers are allergic to certain foods or ingredients, or suffer from juvenile diabetes, and must therefore avoid certain ingredients. Make sure your toddler has regular medical checkups and discuss any special nutritional needs or concerns with your pediatrician.

Chewing and Chopping

It is very exciting when your toddler can chop through a carrot or another hard food all by himself. But with this achievement, it's important to realize choking hazards. Hard foods become more of a choking hazard, not less, when your child sprouts those strong teeth. Be sure to cut crunchy foods to the size of half a grape before serving. Some squishy foods can also pose problems, given the ease with which they can become lodged in youngster's throats. Foods like grapes should be cut in half, and hot dogs and other meats should be served in pieces small enough to be swallowed easily. Even very soft food can be a problem if toddlers stuff their mouths or try to talk while their mouths are full. Discourage them from doing either.

Mommy Must
Just like vegetarian adults, vegetarian toddlers need some extras added to their meals. When cooking for your tot, take special precautions to mix vegetables properly so kids get enough protein, iron, zinc, and B vitamins. Little vegans should also get calcium supplements. Consult your pediatrician for recommendations.

The Joy of Dipping

Meal time is play time, right? And what's better to play with a soupy, yummy liquid that you can dip stuff into? Nothing! Some kids just love sauces, salad dressings, and condiments like ketchup. Many go through a phase of wanting to add ketchup to everything; they think it improves the taste of everything from turkey to cereal! To date, there are no reports of children being adversely affected by this kind of strange culinary preference.

Sauces can encourage toddlers to do a better job on their veggies. But if they are just as happy to eat their foods au naturel, why encourage them to slather on extras that are typically high in salt, chemicals, and fat? Rather than passing on unhealthy family traditions to the next generation, it's better to let them die out. So, before you resort to salad dressing, try a squeeze of lemon and pinch of herbs. Don't boil rice, pasta, or vegetables in salt. Add it after the food is on your toddler's plate, if necessary.

Leisurely Meals

If toddlers take ages to finish a meal, why rush them? The modern trend is to race through a meal—but why? Nowhere is it written that food must be consumed within fifteen minutes. So give them time; enjoy it together! Toddlers need a long time to eat for several reasons. It is challenging for them to get food onto a spoon or fork and into their mouth. Furthermore, they don't have many teeth to chew with, and their poor ability to coordinate the muscles of their faces and mouths makes chewing and swallowing difficult.

And of course, they must pause to enjoy the sensation of eggs sliding through their fingers and the sound of pickles being banged on a plate. Given that all that fingering and mouthing is good for their motor skills and cognitive development, they derive lots of benefit from the assorted activities they indulge in while satisfying their bird-sized appetites. Let them take their time. Otherwise, they may have difficulty consuming enough to keep them well nourished.

To end a marathon meal but still ensure they've had enough to eat, try the following tactics:

- Announce that since he's not eating, the meal is ending, and you're going to take away his plate.
- If he doesn't begin aiming the food toward his mouth on cue, he may not have understood. Demonstrate by removing the plate.
- If he fusses, assume he is still hungry and return his plate to him.
- If he resumes playing instead of eating, offer to feed him. (Until fine motor skills develop, toddlers have trouble getting food into their mouths.)
- If he eats or allows himself to be fed, wait to remove the plate until the next time he begins playing. Then remove it for keeps.
- Offer water if he cries, and reassure him that he will be served again at snack time or the next meal.

Tummy Rumbles

When you want your child to eat and he just refuses, it can be frustrating. If he wants a bag of chips instead of an apple, you may feel annoyed. The point is that feeding your toddler is not an easy task! Below you will find a helpful chart, reminding you the do's and don'ts of mealtime.

Do	Don't
Provide only healthy choices	Offer junk foods
Let children dawdle through their meals	Rush them
Offer to help feed them	Insist on helping
Serve previously refused foods early in a meal	Force them to eat things they don't like when they're hungriest
Offer small portions, and let them know they are free to ask for more	Give large servings and coax them to eat
Make mealtime relaxed and enjoyable	Nag them about eating
Let them eat as little or as much as they want	Play "here comes the airplane" to induce them to open up and eat more

Clever Veggies

Here's a trick that might save a lot of time and energy! Think about it—sugar coatings work to get kids to eat cereal. So why shouldn't it work to get kids to eat veggies, too? As it turns out, it does. If you sprinkle some sugar on broccoli, peas, lettuce—or whatever—

most children will gladly gobble the greens. Once they've developed a taste for the vegetables in question, reduce the amount of sugar added to subsequent servings until it is eliminated altogether.

Cute Concoctions

You don't have to be an artist to be creative! This is the time to go a little crazy with your kid's food—who knows, he may love broccoli if it looks like a tree trunk. It's common for kids to resist the raw carrots, lettuce, alfalfa sprouts, and peas lying on their plates in traditional arrangements, which is to say in small piles. A glob of cottage cheese and smear of peanut butter on bread may not hold much appeal for finicky eaters. But turn those same ingredients into 3-D designs, and toddlers are apt to undergo a dramatic attitude change. Who can resist a figure made of carrot legs, green bean arms, cottage cheese face, raisin eyes, tomato smile, and alfalfa sprout hair lounging amid broccoli trees growing in peanut butter sand anchored in cement—er, crackers? To entice kids to eat good foods, be creative! Here are a few other ideas you can try:

- Cut bread with cookie cutters to create interesting shapes before topping with cheese or vegetables. The leftover bread can be frozen and eventually used to stuff chicken or turkey.
- Slice a banana lengthwise to make a boat; stand a piece of sliced cheese inside to make a sail; and float it in a pool of blueberry yogurt.

You can even infest the water with shark fins made from salami slices. (If that combination doesn't sound appealing to you, remember that your child probably won't mind, and it all ends up in the same place, anyway!)

- Spread strips of toast with cream cheese or peanut butter and top with a row of raisins for an enticing dish of "ants on a log."

Taste Testing, a Whole New World

Keep trying—that's the name of the game. Most children will turn up their noses the first and second times they taste peas, broccoli, and any number of other foods parents consider healthy. After trying again and again, the best recourse, nutritionists say, is for parents to try yet again and again. It can take eight to ten exposures before a youngster develops a taste for a new food!

However, most tots are destined to dislike certain foods. Just as many adults never develop a taste for liver or cringe at the sight of Roquefort dressing, little ones have definite preferences. Other things being equal, one way to tell that a child is in a growth spurt

Mindful Mommy

Offering new foods and encouraging their toddler to take a taste is one kind of "exposure" most parents have used successfully. Heavy-handed tactics like force-feeding are more likely to harden resistance than induce acceptance...and may propel a child toward lifelong eating problems.

is an increase in appetite. While her appetite is hefty, she may be more receptive to new and previously rejected foods. Offer them early in the meal, when she is hungry and less finicky.

Food Struggles

Don't let mealtime turn into something unpleasant. Every mother wants her child to eat enough or the right things, but mealtimes can easily degenerate into food struggles when parents obsess about each pea on their child's plate. If you pay too much attention to exactly what children consume, it's easy for food struggles to develop—and they are notoriously difficult to win. Parents can lead toddlers to vegetables, but even if they tried to force them down their throats, they can't keep them in their stomachs. Overall, the biggest impediment to a well-balanced diet is that bane of modern households: snacking.

I'm Hungry

You will, no doubt, hear "Mommy, I'm hungry!" You might be in the car, in the store, or at your house. It's two hours until dinner time. What do you do? Should she have to wait? If the answer is "yes," you risk sending the message that the clock is more important in determining her need to eat than the signals her tummy is sending. The goal, some nutritionists suggest, should be for toddlers to learn to tune in to their internal hunger cues, not ignore them.

You can offer part of the regular meal in advance, like the salad or vegetables, so the child gets a nutritious snack and a head start on dinner. A child may turn up his nose at the chance to start on his soup before the rest of the family. But if he's hungry, he'll eat it. The trouble begins when the cook prepares special between-meal snacks to satisfy kiddie culinary whims.

Test of Wills

Are you a strong believer in the nothing-until-the-next-regularly-scheduled-meal-or-snack policy? If so, you could soon have a very cranky youngster on your hands. On the other hand, if you always answer his hunger call with a snack, he will get used to getting what he wants. So what are you to do?

If you want to end the test of wills, and put yourself back in charge, you can put your child to bed without his dinner. Children will not die of hunger in one night! Unless they are suffering from diabetes or another disorder, they won't end up nutritionally deficient, either. So if parents don't back down, the problem will be solved when the child sits down to breakfast with bona fide hunger pangs.

Autistic children often have very persistent food obsessions, but although this is rare, it is possible for any exceptionally strong-willed toddler to dig in his heels and reject food despite intense hunger. More often, it is the parents' fear that the child will die of malnutrition before deigning to eat a well-balanced meal that drives them to allow continuing between-meal snacks.

Don't Pass on Your Problems

A March 2001 study in the *Journal of the American Academy of Child and Adolescent Psychiatry* found that mothers with eating disorders were more intrusive with their infants during mealtimes (and during play, too). Toddler weight was found to be related to both the amount of conflict during mealtimes and the mother's preoccupation with her own weight—with lower toddler poundage associated with more conflict and more personal maternal weight worries.

Mealtime is a great time to teach your toddler rules and establish limits. Lessons learned during mealtime can transcend and be used for the bigger-discipline picture. It is especially important to have a balanced approach during mealtimes. Toddlers must be simultaneously nurtured (by being fed) and given firm limits (by restraining them in a high chair and keeping them from throwing food). Balancing the two is a heady emotional experience, and research shows that parents who had highly conflicted relationships with their own parents have a harder time filling both roles.

All the emphasis on food can make the toddler years particularly trying for adults with eating

Mommy Must

Lots of kids books deal with the issue of food. The Very Hungry Caterpillar by Eric Carle is an award-winning book they'll love learning from. Cloudy with a Chance of Meatballs by Judi Barrett will tickle their funny bones as well.

disorders. This is a good time to enter counseling, therapy, or join an Overeaters Anonymous support group to get some real culinary help.

No Sweets

Some parents are determined never to allow candy to pass their children's lips so they won't develop a taste for sweets. What a feat! Unfortunately, this strategy can backfire by imbuing creamy, crunchy, gooey, sugary foods with the heady mystique of the forbidden.

Although palates differ, anthropologists believe that the human love of sweets is inborn. Apparently our taste buds were designed to guide primitive humans toward edible, calorie-rich plants (typically sweet) and away from poisonous ones (generally bitter).

When you think about it this way, it seems almost impossible to keep kids away from sweets. Unless children are being raised on a desert island, sooner or later they will discover the wonders of cakes, candy bars, cookies, and pies. And if they have a normal set of taste buds, they will probably love them.

If a bank teller or doctor's receptionist offers your toddler a lollipop, jumping in to forbid the gift in the absence of a compelling reason may be exerting the kind of control that causes youngsters to work overtime to satisfy their inborn sweet tooth. (A compelling reason to step in would be if the child has a medical problem, such as diabetes or an allergy.) Certainly it is reasonable to insist toddlers wait to consume their gift until later. In doing so, parents may teach the most important lesson: it's okay to eat sweets at certain times. It's when they're consumed just "whenever" that they become a problem.

At least, that is the generally accepted wisdom from experts in the toddler nutrition field: monitor the consumption of "junk foods" at home and accept that standards will be lower outside of it.

Strange Cravings

So you're trying to be open, available to your little one. You've made him this, that, and the other thing, just to see what he likes. But now he wants to eat something that's not food! What do you do? It's true, some youngsters actually consume materials not meant to be ingested—this is called pica. Pica is a craving for unnatural foods or items such as soil, paint, string, cloth, hair—even feces and animal droppings. Pica does not usually signal a deficiency of vitamins and minerals. It is most prevalent among mentally retarded youngsters, but can develop among otherwise normal youngsters, too. It typically occurs in children age eighteen months to two years, and parents must monitor these youngsters carefully to prevent them from satisfying their strange cravings.

Smart Mommy

Toddlers, like adults, will eat out of boredom. If the parent responds to request for a snack by offering several healthy alternatives but the child refuses anything but a cookie, she's probably not hungry. An appealing activity or nap may do a better job of eliminating the crankiness.

Pica usually only lasts a few months before disappearing on its own.

Something else to keep in mind is rumination disorder. Children with rumination disorder vomit their food into their mouths without signs of nausea or retching or stomach upset. They may eject it from their mouths, or proceed to chew it again and swallow it without signs of disgust. It occurs most commonly among children with Sandifer's syndrome, esophageal reflux, and mental retardation, typically beginning between three and twelve months. Consult your pediatrician if your child shows signs of these disorders.

High Chairs and Booster Seats

Your child will be spending a lot of time in his high chair or booster seat. It is important that you buy him a safe one! There are a lot of things to keep in mind when you travel to the store and set up the seat at home. First and foremost, when purchasing a high chair, choose one with a wide base, since that adds stability. Other ways to keep toddlers safe are:

- Position high chairs away from hazards, such as stoves, windows, and drapery cords.
- Don't allow the child to stand in the chair unsupervised. (If the chair tips or the child loses his balance and falls, it's a long way to the ground head first.)

- Use the safety belt rather than relying on the tray to hold the child in.
- Be sure the tray is properly latched on both sides, as babies tend to push against the tray when seated.
- Periodically check for loose screws and a wobbly base.

Magazines or old telephone books wrapped in contact paper make adequate booster seats, although their lack of a safety belt makes them useless for youngsters who refuse to remain seated. Buying one for everyday use so that older toddlers can sit at the table has some advantages. Tending to toddlers can be easier when they are sitting at the same level, then adults can eat with fewer distractions. Putting the child's plate and cup on a tray can help contain the mess, and being on the same level with everyone else makes her feel more like part of the family. As she mimics those around her, her behavior, manners, and even food choices may improve.

Mommy Must

Applesauce, milk, and tomatoes dribbling down your toddler's legs will eventually land on your floor. Until her aim improves to the point where most of the food ends up in her mouth, spread a few newspapers or a drop cloth under her high chair to cut down on cleanup.

Restaurant Survival

Sometime you just have to get out of the house for a meal. Whether the babysitter cancelled or you want to introduce your tot to an old friend, toddlers can make very unpleasant dining companions in restaurants! Remember that it's not his fault; dining out requires two skills your child might not have mastered yet: sitting and waiting. If you take your son or daughter to a place designed for adults, it is apt to be a miserable experience for the parents, the child, and other patrons as well.

You can minimize upsets, however, by arriving prepared. In general, the fancier the restaurant, the longer the wait; so if the cupboard in your diaper bag is bare, don't even wait for the waiter— as you're being seated, ask the host to bring bread or crackers posthaste. It's a good idea to arrive with entertainment, too. Try to bring something new and different; otherwise, the novelty of items on the table will hold much more appeal. Rather than beginning the litany of no-no's the minute a small hand gravitates toward a coffee cup, scan the table for items your toddler can safely play with. Trying to prevent youngsters from touching anything guarantees a series of noisy scenes. Toddlers simply must have something to do, so be realistic. Allow them to bang a spoon if there's a tablecloth to dampen the sound or to shred a napkin.

Given the challenge of coping with toddlers in standard establishments, it's better to stick to kid-friendly restaurants. Many places have been specially designed for families with tots. Unfortunately, they often come up short in the nutrition department, but areas for climbing and crawling offer some compensation by offering opportunities to practice their physical skills. Parents shouldn't expect to relax while toddlers entertain themselves, however. Most structures are overly challenging for tots, and if bigger kids are roughhousing, play areas can be outright dangerous. Close monitoring is imperative. If a sign forbids children under a certain height from entering an area, believe it! On the other hand, ignore the signs prohibiting big people from entering if your toddler is in a potentially dangerous situation. Climb on in and stage a rescue!

Mindful Mommy

Don't let everyone in the restaurant know that you are trying to avoid a fit or tantrum. Try to keep your voice down when chastising your toddler. Parental nagging is often louder and more incessant than an occasional whine from a toddler, and hence more disruptive to other patrons.

Part 2

Recipes for a Happy and Healthy Toddler

Chapter 3

From Baby to Toddler

REMEMBER THAT THE GOAL of feeding in the first year is mostly about getting your baby used to different tastes and textures. Breastmilk or formula will still provide most of the calories and other nutrients to your baby's diet through the first year.

9–12 Months

On the following pages you will find various recipes for cooking for your young toddler. During this transitional phase, make sure to keep it simple and slow. Kids will learn to eat, as long as they get the right foods and have support along the way!

Steamy Zucchini

3 SERVINGS

½ medium zucchini
2 cups water

1. Wash the zucchini thoroughly. Trim off the ends, then cut the zucchini into ¼-inch slices.
2. Place in a steamer basket inside a medium saucepan. Fill the pot with water until it reaches the bottom of the steamer basket.
3. Bring to a boil, then steam for 10–15 minutes, or until tender.
4. Cut each slice into quarters, and serve as finger food.

Zucchini

Summer is a great time to introduce your baby to new vegetables, especially zucchini! Soft, tender, and tasty, this vegetable can be found in abundance at local markets. It's easy to grow, too—try planting some in your garden next summer.

Beloved Baked Winter Squash

2 SERVINGS

¼ medium winter squash
2 cups water

1. Wash the squash thoroughly. Cut it open and scoop out the seeds.
2. Place face-down in a shallow pan of water. Bake at 400°F for 45 minutes, or until squash is tender, but still slightly firm.
3. Remove from oven and allow to cool completely.
4. Cut small cubes of squash from the shell, and serve to baby as finger food.

Winter Squash Versus Summer Squash

Winter squashes make a great finger food. They're denser than summer squashes like zucchini, and hold up better when grabbed by little hands. Texture-wise, they're more similar to a carrot than a melon, and babies with a few teeth will probably handle winter squash better than their toothless friends.

Steamed Summery Squash

2 SERVINGS

½ medium summer squash (such as yellow crook-
  neck, pattipan, or others)
2 cups water

1. Wash the squash thoroughly. Cut off ends, and
   cut into 1–2-inch chunks.
2. Place in a saucepan with a small amount of
   water. Steam until tender, about 10 minutes.
3. Drain the squash pieces and place in a food processor or blender. Purée until mixture is smooth,
   adding water, breastmilk, or formula as necessary. Or serve as a finger food.

Look Ma, I Ate the Whole Thing!

Summer squash is similar to zucchini because the
entire vegetable is edible. Choose a squash with few
surface blemishes, scrub it well with a vegetable
brush, and you can feed the entire vegetable to babies
about 8 months and older. If it doesn't purée smoothly
enough for your baby, use a vegetable peeler to remove
the soft skin next time.

Perfectly Steamed Peas

1 SERVING

½ cup fresh or frozen peas
1 cup water

1. Place washed peas in a steamer basket. Put basket in a saucepan with about 2 inches of water.
2. Bring to a boil, then steam for about 10 minutes or until peas are tender.
3. Let peas cool before serving.

Peas

Peas are a great finger food, but watch your baby carefully to make sure she can move them around in her mouth. When in doubt, mash with a fork before serving.

Great Steamy Green Beans

3 SERVINGS

15 green beans
2 cups water

1. Wash the beans thoroughly. Trim the ends off, removing the strings.
2. Place in a steamer basket inside a medium saucepan. Fill the pot with water until it reaches the bottom of the steamer basket.
3. Bring to a boil, then steam for 10–15 minutes, or until tender.
4. Cut each bean into quarters, and serve as finger food.

Green Bean Side Dishes

When beans are in season, buy and prepare them in bulk. Steam up a couple of pounds at a time. Reserve some for baby, and try serving the rest with slivered almonds. You could also make a cold green bean salad by sautéeing with garlic, olive oil, and red peppers. Green bean casserole is another family favorite.

Amazing Steamy Apples

4 SERVINGS

1 medium apple
½ cup water

1. Wash the apple. Peel and core it, then cut into thin slices.
2. Place in a saucepan with a small amount of water. Steam until tender, about 10 minutes.
3. Drain the apple pieces and serve as finger food.

First Finger Foods

Once baby is about 9 months old, it's the perfect time to introduce more finger foods. Some babies have a tendency to shove everything into their mouths at once, so be extremely vigilant while your little ones eat. Soft vegetables should be small enough to be picked up, but not large enough to cause choking.

Pleasantly Steamy Pears

4 SERVINGS

1 medium pear
½ cup water

1. Wash the pear. Peel and core it, then cut into thin slices.
2. Place in a saucepan with a small amount of water. Steam until tender, about 10 minutes.
3. Drain the pear slices and serve as finger food.

Slippery Food

If baby's tender apples and pears slip right through her fingers, crush a bowlful of oat ring cereal (like Cheerios) into powder, and lightly dust her fruits and vegetables with it before serving. Baby's fingers will adhere better to the fruit, so more of it makes it into her tummy.

Slow Cooker, Worth the Wait, Applesauce

10 SERVINGS

5–6 medium apples
1 teaspoon cinnamon
¼ cup sugar, optional
1 teaspoon lemon juice
½ cup water

1. Wash, peel, and core the apples. Cut into chunks.
2. Combine all ingredients in the slow cooker. Set on low.
3. Cook for about 8 hours, stirring every hour or so, until the apples are completely cooked.
4. If the applesauce is still chunkier than you'd like, run it through a food processor or blender.

Apple Replacements

No apples to be found? You can make slow cooker fruit sauce from just about anything that's in season—pears, peaches, plums, etc. Just adjust the cooking time as necessary; ripe pears, for example, won't take as long to cook as firm apples.

Perfectly Steamy Plums

2 SERVINGS

1 ripe plum
1 cup water

1. Wash the plum. Peel and remove the pit, then cut into thin slices.
2. If the plum is already ripe and very soft to the touch, you're done!
3. If the plum still feels firm, place in a steamer basket in a saucepan. Add enough water so that it fills the pot under the steamer basket.
4. Bring to a boil and then steam until tender, about 5–8 minutes.
5. Let the plum slices cool, and then serve as finger food.

Plums

There is a wide variety of plums available in the summer months. Choose from many of the European varieties grown in the United States, which can range in color from green to red to purplish-blue. Don't forget about the approximately 15 different types of Japanese plums, too!

Mashed Duo: Apricots and Pears

3 SERVINGS

1 medium pear
2 ripe apricots
2 cups water

1. Wash, peel, and core the pear. Cut into chunks and place in steamer basket.
2. Wash, halve, and remove pit from the apricots. Place along with pear chunks in steamer basket.
3. Add enough water so that it fills the pot under the steamer basket. Bring to a boil and steam for 10 minutes, or until apricots are very soft.
4. Remove skins from apricots by scooping the fruit out with a spoon. Place on a plate along with the pear, and fork-mash fruit together.

How to Skin a 'cot

Apricots are fairly difficult to peel because their tender fruit is likely to peel off along with the skin! A good technique is to steam the apricot first, then slide a fork or spoon along the inner edge of the peel to remove the fruit. This technique also works on peaches, tomatoes, and other juicy fruits.

Magic Mashed Pears and Spinach

4 SERVINGS

1 medium pear   *2 cups fresh spinach*
2 cups water

1. Wash, peel, and core the pear. Cut into chunks and place in a steamer basket, then place the basket inside a saucepan.
2. Add water to fill the bottom of the saucepan. Bring to a boil and steam until pear is very tender, about 8–10 minutes.
3. Boil washed spinach in a pan of shallow water for about 10 minutes.
4. If using frozen spinach, defrost and cook according to the package directions. You'll need about ½ cup cooked spinach for this recipe.
5. Place the spinach and pears on a plate along with the pear, and fork-mash them together. Add leftover cooking water from the pear if the mixture is too thick.

Spinach

Spinach is definitely a powerhouse food. If your baby balks, tell her the story of Popeye, the cartoon sailor from 1929 who was able to do the work of twelve men because he ate his spinach. Your rendition of a sailor dance might also help convince her of the merits of eating spinach!

Marvelously Mashed Peaches and Sweet Potatoes

3 SERVINGS

1 medium ripe peach
½ small sweet potato

1. Scrub the sweet potato and poke several holes in it. Bake at 400°F for 40 minutes.
2. Wash the peach and cut in half. Remove the pit and any of the harder inner fruit.
3. Scoop the peach out of the peel, or remove the peel with a paring knife. Place on a large plate.
4. When the sweet potato is cool, scoop the potato out of the peel. Combine on plate with peach, and fork-mash together.
5. Mashing the peach may release more juice that you need, causing the meal to become too runny. Drain off the juice as required, and continue mashing until the mixture has a fairly smooth consistency.

Peaches

Peaches and sweet potatoes make for a very colorful meal. Many babies like the bright colors in this recipe and may want to feed it to themselves. If so, try using a bowl with a suction cup on the bottom so that it won't slide off baby's high chair tray, and give baby a rubber- or plastic-coated spoon so she won't hurt her gums.

Perfectly Puréed Vegetables
with Chicken

4 SERVINGS

1 medium carrot
1 small white potato
½ cup cooked chicken
2 cups water

1. Wash and peel the carrot. Cut into coin-sized dices and place in a saucepan. Wash and peel the potato. Cut into small cubes and add to the saucepan.
2. Add enough water to cover the vegetables. Bring to a boil, then cook for 15–20 minutes or until the vegetables are very tender.
3. Remove all fat, skin, and bones from chicken. Dice.
4. Remove vegetables and place on plate along with chicken. Fork-mash until it reaches a consistency suitable for your baby. Or purée in a food processor or food mill to produce a smoother texture.
5. Add breastmilk or formula, one teaspoon at a time, to make the mixture smoother.

Scrape It Down

If you're using a full-sized food processor to purée ¼ cup vegetables and meat, don't be surprised if your ingredients all stick to the sides of the processor bowl. Stop the processor every few seconds to scrape down the sides, pushing all the food back into the blades.

Puréed, and Terrific, Turkey and Cranberries

4 SERVINGS

½ cup cooked turkey
½ cup fresh cranberries
1 tablespoon sugar
¼ cup water

1. Mix the water and sugar in a saucepan. Bring to a boil and cook at a high temperature for 2–3 minutes, stirring constantly.
2. Add cranberries. Reduce heat to a simmer, then cook for 15–20 minutes. Cranberries should burst, and the mixture will thicken.
3. Allow cranberries to cool completely.
4. Dice turkey. Mix with cranberries and fork-mash together until they reach a consistency your baby will accept. You can also purée the mixture in food processor or food mill.
5. Add breastmilk or formula, one teaspoon at a time, to make the mixture smoother.

Cranberries

Just about any kind of cranberries can be used for this recipe. If you don't want to use fresh ones, the canned varieties are fine—jellied cranberries won't even need cooking or puréeing before serving. If using canned whole-berry cranberries, run the berries through a blender or food processor before serving.

Spectacular Puréed Spinach with Pasta

3 SERVINGS

¼ cup thin pasta
1 cup fresh or frozen spinach
2 cups water

1. Place pasta in a pot and cover with water. Boil for 20–25 minutes, or until pasta is very tender.
2. If using fresh spinach, wash the leaves thoroughly, remove stems, and chop. Boil in a pan of shallow water for 10 minutes. If using frozen spinach, defrost and cook according to the package directions.
3. Combine the cooked spinach and pasta in a food processor or blender. Purée for about 30 seconds.
4. Add breastmilk or formula, one tablespoon at a time. Continue puréeing until the mixture reaches a creamy consistency.

Pasta Differences

For the purpose of puréed baby food, try to use a pasta that cooks up soft, such as tubular or ribbon noodles. Like your spaghetti al dente? Overcook it for baby, since chewy or hard noodles will not purée well. Also avoid whole wheat pastas—they may be healthier, but usually have a firmer consistency.

Yummy Chicken and Sweet Potatoes

4 SERVINGS

1 small sweet potato
1 small boneless, skinless chicken breast (about 6 oz)

1. Wash the sweet potato, remove the skin, and cut into cubes. Place in a pot and cover with water.
2. Bring the water to a boil, then cook for about 25 minutes or until potato is completely tender. Save the cooking liquid.
3. Place the chicken in a separate small saucepan, and cover with water. Bring to a boil and cook for about 20 minutes, or until the internal temperature reaches 170°F.
4. After both chicken and potato have cooled, combine in food processor or blender. Pulse for 30 seconds.
5. Add breastmilk or formula, one tablespoon at a time, to make the mixture smoother. Continue puréeing until smooth.

Pasty Purée

Are your chicken-based purées coming out either too chunky or too pasty? Try adding a little bit of butter or margarine if baby is older than 6 months. It may smooth out the mixture just enough to please even a fussy eater. If your child is sensitive to dairy products, try a non-dairy margarine.

Chicken and Peach Creation

4 SERVINGS

½ cup cooked chicken
¼ cup white or brown rice, cooked
½ very ripe peach

1. Slice the peach in half, removing the pit and any hard parts around the pit
2. Using a spoon, scoop the peach flesh out of the skin. Mash with a fork, then drain the leftover juice into a small dish.
3. Dice chicken. Add to a plate with the peach.
4. Add rice. Fork-mash until the mixture is well-combined.
5. Add the leftover peach juice as necessary to thin the mash. If it's still too thick, add either extra peach juice, breastmilk, or formula, one tablespoon at a time, to make the mixture smoother. Continue mashing until smooth. Alternatively, purée in food processor for a smoother consistency.

Apricots and Peaches

Like peaches, apricots are stone fruits that, when ripe, have a very high moisture content. That means when you're fork-mashing, expect juice to come running out. Peach recipes can generally use apricots as a substitute, but make sure to double or triple the amount of fruit, because apricots are considerably smaller than peaches.

Terrific Trio:
Chicken, Carrots, and Rice

4 SERVINGS

½ cup cooked chicken
¼ cup cooked white or brown rice
1 medium carrot

1. Wash and peel the carrots. Cut into small pieces.
2. Place in a saucepan with enough water to cover the carrots. Bring the water to a boil, then simmer until the carrots are very tender, about 15–20 minutes
3. Place the carrots in a food processor or blender with the rice.
4. Dice chicken. Add to the food processor, and purée for 30 seconds.
5. Add water, breastmilk, or formula, one tablespoon at a time, to make the mixture smoother. Continue puréeing until smooth.

The Best Liquid

While water is an effective thinner, you can also use homemade chicken or vegetable stock, if baby has already tried them. Don't use them in combination recipes until you're sure that they are well-tolerated, and avoid store-bought bouillons, which contain a lot of salt and other spices.

Nourishing Beef, Squash, and Pasta

3 SERVINGS

½ cup cooked beef
¼ small butternut squash
¼ cup cooked pasta

1. Remove the seeds from the squash. Place face-down in a shallow pan of water. Bake for about 40 minutes at 400°F.
2. Allow to cool, then scoop out the squash flesh and place in food processor or blender. Chop the beef into small pieces, and add to food processor. Add pasta.
3. Purée as needed to reach desired consistency. Add water, breastmilk, or formula, 1 tablespoon at a time, to thin out the mixture.

Combining Foods

Don't be afraid to try new food combinations for your baby. By combining a meat, a starch, and a vegetable, you can get a complete meal in each spoonful!

Best Beef, Peas, and Potatoes

3 SERVINGS

½ cup cooked beef
½ cup peas (fresh or frozen)
1 small potato (or ½ large potato)

1. Wash, peel, and dice potato. Place in a saucepan, cover with water, and boil for 10–15 minutes.
2. Add peas to saucepan. Boil for another 5–10 minutes until peas and potatoes are both very tender.
3. Let cool, then place in food processor with beef. Purée as needed to reach desired consistency, adding leftover cooking water to thin out the mixture.

Pasta Flours

Pasta dough is usually made of unbleached white flour or semolina flour, but you can find it made with just about any grain: oat flour, corn flour, buckwheat flour, or even mung bean threads. If your baby has a wheat allergy, try substituting standard pasta with one made of these alternate flours.

Chummy Chicken, Carrots, and Green Beans

4 SERVINGS

½ cup cooked chicken
½ cup green beans
   (fresh or frozen)

1 cup water
1 medium carrot

1. Wash and peel the carrot. Cut. Place in a saucepan with enough water to cover the carrot pieces. Bring the water to a boil, then simmer until tender, about 10 minutes.
2. Break off the ends of the green beans (if fresh) and pull the strings off the sides. Cut into small pieces.
3. Add the green beans to the partially cooked carrots; add more water if necessary to cover. Cook for another 10 minutes or so, until both are tender.
4. Purée carrots, beans, and chicken for 30 seconds.
5. Add chicken, breastmilk, or formula, one tablespoon at a time, to smooth. Continue puréeing until smooth.

Green Beans

Green beans are a great source of vitamin C. Make sure to remove all the strings from them before cooking, otherwise the beans will be too fibrous to purée well and will cause your baby problems when she tries to eat them.

Terrific Trio:
Pork, Green Beans, and Potatoes

4 SERVINGS

½ cup cooked pork, chopped
½ cup green beans (fresh or frozen)
1 cup water
1 small potato (or ½ large potato)

1. Wash and peel the potato. Cut into small pieces.
2. Break off the ends of the green beans (if fresh) and pull the strings off the sides. Cut into small pieces. Place in the saucepan with the potato pieces.
3. Add enough water to cover the potato and string bean pieces. Bring the water to a boil, then simmer until the potatoes and beans are very tender, about 15 minutes.
4. Place the beans, potatoes, and pork in a food processor or blender and purée for 30 seconds.
5. Add cooking water, breastmilk, or formula, one tablespoon at a time, to make the mixture smoother. Continue puréeing until smooth.

Foods Made with Breastmilk

Unlike mixtures made with cow's milk or formula, foods thinned with breastmilk tends to get thinner over time if they sit because the natural compounds in breastmilk, such as lipase, tend to break down the food and cause it to become thinner. This means that it's better to mix foods with breastmilk right before serving them.

Chicken Stew with Barley, Yum

5 SERVINGS

1 small chicken breast (about 4 ounces)
1 small white potato
1 medium carrot
¼ cup cooked barley
1 cup water

1. Wash the chicken and cut into 1-inch pieces. Place in a saucepan. Cover with water and bring to a boil, and cook for about 10 minutes.
2. Wash, peel, and slice the carrot into ½-inch chunks. Add to the cooking pot.
3. Wash, peel, and chop the potato into ½-inch cubes. Add to the cooking pot, and continue cooking until everything is completely cooked and tender, about 20–25 minutes longer.
4. Once cooled, place the stewed ingredients into a food processor, along with the cooked barley. Purée until smooth, adding breastmilk or formula as needed to thin it out.

A Starch Is a Starch Is a Starch . . .

When it comes to baby food, you can generally substitute one starch for another without hearing any complaints. If you don't have any white potatoes on hand, substitute half of a sweet potato or yam. If you happen to have leftover rice from last night's dinner, use that instead.

Fruity Chicken Stew

5 SERVINGS

I small boneless, skin-
less chicken breast
(about 4 ounces)
½ medium apple

½ very ripe peach
1 medium carrot
½ cup cooked rice
1 cup water

1. Wash the chicken, cut into 1-inch pieces, and
   place in a saucepan. Cover with water and bring
   to a boil, and cook for about 10 minutes.
2. Wash, peel, and slice the carrot into ½-inch
   chunks. Add to the cooking pot.
3. Wash, peel, and chop the apple into ½-inch
   cubes. Add to the cooking pot, and continue
   cooking until everything is completely cooked
   and tender, about 20–25 minutes longer.
4. Wash the peach and remove the pit and skin. Dice.
5. Once cooled, place the stewed ingredients into
   a food processor, along with the cooked rice and
   diced peach. Purée until smooth, adding breastmilk or formula as needed to thin it out.

But My Peaches Aren't Ripe!

If peaches aren't quite in season or the ones you
have aren't especially ripe, don't despair. Boiling or
steaming for 10–15 minutes should soften them up
enough for either puréeing or fork-mashing. Use the
same trick for other stone fruits (such as apricots
and plums). Remember that they won't be as sweet as
naturally ripe fruit.

Unbelievable Banana Oatmeal

2 SERVINGS

¼ cup regular oats (not quick-cooking)
½ very ripe banana
1 cup water

1. Grind the oats into a powder, using either a food processor or blender. Alternatively, a mortar and pestle makes a terrific grinder for a small amount.
2. Pour water into a small saucepan. Bring to a rolling boil. Add the powdered oats into the boiling water, stirring constantly for about 30 seconds.
3. Cover the pot, turn down the heat to low and simmer for 8–10 minutes, or until the oats are smooth and thick. Stir occasionally to prevent sticking and burning.
4. Peel the banana, removing any brown spots. Fork-mash on a plate until completely creamed.
5. Mix the banana with the cooled cereal. Add breastmilk or formula to thin, if necessary.

Oatmeal

As soon as baby's had her first oatmeal and shows no sign of allergies, mix it up! Banana oatmeal is a great early cereal because it combines two of the foods that are easiest to digest: cereal and bananas.

Perfectly Pear Oatmeal

2 SERVINGS

¼ *cup regular oats (not quick-cooking)*
½ *very ripe pear*
1 *cup water*

1. Grind the oats into a powder, using either a food processor or blender. Alternatively, a mortar and pestle makes a terrific grinder for a small amount.
2. Pour the water into a small saucepan. Bring to a rolling boil. Add the powdered oats into the boiling water, stirring constantly for about 30 seconds.
3. Cover the pot, turn down the heat to low and simmer for 8–10 minutes, or until the oats are smooth and thick. Stir occasionally to prevent sticking and burning.
4. Remove the core and skin from the pear. Dice into pieces, and then fork-mash on a plate until completely smooth.
5. Mix the pear with the cooled cereal.

Rib-Stickin' Good?

A hearty bowl of oatmeal is supposed to stick to the ribs, right? If you feed baby oatmeal for breakfast, does that mean she'll be satiated until lunchtime? Not on your life! Most babies will snack every couple of hours, regardless of what they've just eaten.

Swedish Teething Cookies

10 SERVINGS

1 cup all-purpose flour
1 cup graham flour or
  rye flour
2 tablespoons sugar
½ teaspoon baking soda
½ teaspoon baking
  powder

1 cup cornmeal
3 tablespoons marga-
  rine or vegetable
  shortening
¾ cup milk, water,
  or soy milk

1. Preheat oven to 350°F. Mix together all dry ingredients. Cut in margarine or shortening with two forks or pastry blender until the mixture resembles fine crumbs.
2. Add liquid and mix well.
3. Roll dough out ½-inch thick and cut into shapes (rectangles are easy for baby to grasp, but also try circles, crescents, or other shapes if desired).
4. Bake for 10–15 minutes until hard and brown.

Knackbrod

This version of Swedish hard bread, called Knack-brod, is intended to crumble slowly in baby's mouth as she gnaws on it. The melt-in-the-mouth consistency is perfect for teething.

Fantastic Banana Apple Farina

4 SERVINGS

3 tablespoons farina
½ cup unsweetened applesauce
½ very ripe banana
1 cup water

1. Bring the water to a boil. Add farina and stir well.
2. Reduce heat and cook until the farina thickens , about 1–3 minutes, stirring continuously. Remove from the heat and allow to cool for about 10 minutes.
3. Peel banana, removing any brown spots. Fork-mash until completely creamed.
4. Stir the applesauce and banana into the cooled cereal.

Where Do I Find Farina?

Baby rice and baby oatmeal are common staples in the neighborhood grocery store. Farina, though, may be a little more difficult to find. Try looking in the hot cereal aisle, next to quick-cooking oats and other breakfast cereals.

Homemade Mighty-Biter Biscuits

20 SERVINGS

⅔ cup milk or water
4 tablespoons butter, melted and cooled, or
  vegetable oil
1 tablespoon brown sugar
1 cup wheat germ (toasted or untoasted)
1 cup whole-wheat flour

1. Beat together milk or water, butter or oil, and sugar.
2. Stir in wheat germ and flour, and knead for 8–10 minutes until dough is smooth and satiny. Add more water or more flour if necessary.
3. Make small balls of dough and roll them into sticks that are about ½-inch thick and 4 inches long.
4. Roll out on floured surface to ½-inch thickness.
5. Bake on a greased cookie sheet at 350°F for 45 minutes, or until the biscuits are hard and browned.

Teething Biscuit Safety

Wait until your baby can comfortably eat solid puréed foods before offering her a teething biscuit. Always supervise your baby carefully while she's eating one—ideally she'll gnaw on the hard biscuit, getting relief for her sore gums while eating some of it, very slowly, in the process. But it's always possible that she could break off a piece big enough to choke on, so be careful.

Homemade Graham Crackers

10 SERVINGS

1 cup graham or whole-wheat flour	1 teaspoon salt
1 cup unbleached flour	½ cup sugar
1 teaspoon baking powder	¼ cup margarine, butter, or shortening
	⅓ cup milk or water

1. Combine flours, salt, baking powder, and sugar.
2. Cut in butter, margarine, or shortening until dough has consistency of cornmeal.
3. Add milk or water and knead to make a stiff dough. Dough will be very crumbly—press together. Roll out on floured surface to a ½-inch thickness.
4. Cut into squares and prick with a fork. Brush with milk or water, if desired.
5. Bake at 400°F for 15–20 minutes, or until golden brown. Separate squares and loosen from pan, but leave on baking sheet to cool.

Graham

Graham flour is a coarser version of whole-wheat flour that includes more of the nutrient-rich parts of the wheat kernel. Graham flour can spoil quickly, so store it in your refrigerator and use within 2–3 months. You can also substitute regular whole-wheat flour in this recipe, but it won't have the full nutty taste of graham crackers.

Baby Cereal Cookie Creations

10 SERVINGS

1 cup all-purpose flour
1 cup baby cereal (rice, oatmeal, etc.)
1 cup apple juice

1. Mix all ingredients well, adding more flour or baby cereal if necessary to achieve a doughlike consistency. Dough will be sticky.
2. Roll dough out to ½-inch thick and cut into sticks about 1-inch wide and 3-inches thick.
3. Bake at 350°F for 20–30 minutes, or until dry and hard.

Other Great Teething Foods

In addition to the array of teething foods presented here, there are other great items that your child may enjoy teething on that may soothe her sore gums. One option is a frozen washcloth—simply run a clean washcloth under cold water and pop it in the freezer. No choking hazards, and baby will at least be momentarily amused by her cold "snack."

Whole-Wheat, Terrific, Teething Crackers

10 SERVINGS

3 cups oatmeal	3 tablespoons sugar
1 cup whole-wheat flour	1 teaspoon salt, optional
1 cup unbleached white flour	¾ cup oil
1 cup wheat germ	1 cup water

1. Preheat oven to 350°F. Mix together oatmeal, flours, wheat germ, and sugar. Beat together oil and water, and work into dry ingredients to form a soft dough. Roll dough onto 2 cookie sheets, sprinkle with salt.
2. Cut dough into squares with knife or pizza cutter.
3. Bake crackers for 15 minutes. Then, check every 3–5 minutes to remove any that are baked. Cool on rack, then store tightly covered.

What a Mess!

Don't be surprised when your child gets more of a teething biscuit on her face, hands, and clothes than she does in her mouth! While different biscuits have different consistencies, the basic idea is that the hard biscuit soothes your child's gums, while dissolving slowly. Once your baby starts getting larger pieces of the biscuit off, it's time to do some cleanup.

Zwieback Toast

12 SERVINGS

1 pkg active dry yeast
¼ cup warm water
½ cup plus 1 table-
    spoon sugar
4 cups all-purpose flour

2 egg yolks
¼ cup margarine or
    butter, melted
1 cup milk, water, or
    soy milk

1. Pour the yeast, 1 tablespoon of flour, and 1 table-spoon sugar into the warm water. Mix until dissolved, then allow it to sit for 10–15 minutes.
2. Add 2 cups of flour and 1 cup of milk to the yeast. Stir to dissolve, then let rest for 5 minutes.
3. Add remaining ingredients, mixing thoroughly. Place in a greased bowl and allow to rise for about 2 hours. Punch down and knead for about 5 minutes.
4. Place 3-inch dough balls on a greased baking sheet and allow to rise for another 2 hours.
5. Bake at 375°F for 20 minutes; let cool; cut into ½-inch slices. Bake again until browned, 20–30 minutes.

Isn't There an Easier Way?

A quick Zwieback toast can be made by simply taking a slice of whole-wheat bread, cutting it into ½-inch slices, and popping it into the oven. Bake at 250°F for 1 hour, or until the toasts are hard. Be sure not to cook at too high a temperature (or too near the top of the oven), or the Zwieback will burn.

Baby Teething Biscotti

8–10 SERVINGS

1 cup all-purpose flour
2 tablespoons brown sugar
½ teaspoon baking powder
¼ teaspoon baking soda
1 egg yolk
1 tablespoon oil
⅓ cup milk, water, or soy milk

1. Mix together flour, sugar, and baking powder.
2. Add egg yolk, oil, and milk. Stir until the mixture forms a firm dough.
3. Shape the dough into a log about 6 inches long. Place on a greased cookie sheet, and press the log into a bar about 2 inches wide. Bake at 325°F for 20 minutes, then cool until the log is cool enough to touch.
4. Cut diagonally into ½-inch slices. Spread out on the cookie sheet, then bake for another 10–15 minutes. Slices should be crispy and dry.
5. Cool on wire racks.

Egg Whites

Baby shouldn't have egg whites until she is at least 1 year old; older babies can better digest egg white protein, and it also will lessen the chance of an egg allergy developing. Egg yolks can start to be given at 6–8 months, so be sure you're using only the yolks in these biscuit recipes.

Homemade Whole-Fat (yah!) Yogurt

8 SERVINGS

1 quart whole milk
⅓ cup nonfat dry milk powder
¼ cup commercial unflavored, cultured yogurt
    (or ¼ cup homemade yogurt)
3 tablespoons sugar

1. Select heat-safe container(s) for finished yogurt, either a 5-cup container or individual smaller containers, and fill with boiling water to keep warm. Preheat oven to 200°F and turn off. Monitor oven temperature with oven thermometer and turn on periodically to keep temperature at 108°F–112°F.

2. Place cold milk in top of double boiler. Stir in nonfat dry milk powder and sugar. Heat milk to 200°F. Measure temperature using a candy thermometer. Hold at this temperature for 10 minutes, stirring gently. Do not boil.

Yogurt

Making your own whole-fat yogurt is a bit complicated, but the results are great. You'll need a small amount of commercial yogurt as a "starter," but once you start making your own yogurt, you can save a bit to start the next batch and just replenish the commercial starter every 5 batches or so.

3. Remove the top of the double boiler and place in cold water. Monitor temperature and cool rapidly to 112°F–115°F. Remove pan from cold water once it reaches this temperature.

4. Remove 1 cup of warm milk from the pan and blend the yogurt starter culture with it. Add to rest of warm milk. Temperature should be 110°F–112°F. Pour yogurt immediately into pre-warmed container(s). Cover and place in oven. Incubate in oven for 4 hours, monitoring temperature and turning oven on and off as needed to keep between 108°F –112°F.

5. Refrigerate yogurt immediately. Yogurt will keep in refrigerator for up to 10 days. Save a small amount as the starter for your next batch of yogurt.

Starting Dairy Products

Once your baby is about 9 months old, she'll be ready for cultured dairy products. Yogurt is a great first dairy product to start with because the active cultures in it will help your baby digest the milk better. This is why your baby can have yogurt and cheese before she's 1 year old, but needs to wait until after 1 year before having plain cow's milk.

Scrumptious Sesame Teething Crackers

12 SERVINGS

¾ cup all-purpose flour
¼ cup whole-wheat flour
2 tablespoons oil
2 tablespoons fresh sesame seeds
¼ cup milk, water, or soy milk
¼ teaspoon salt, optional

1. Preheat oven to 350°F. Mix the flours and oil together in a bowl. Add sesame seeds and stir well.
2. Add water and continue mixing; the dough should reach a slightly sticky consistency.
3. Place dough on a lightly floured surface. Roll to about a ⅛-inch thickness, and cut into 1-inch strips.
4. Bake on an ungreased cookie sheet for 20–25 minutes, or until the crackers are brown and crispy.

Sesame

Sesame is a fun new taste for baby, and probably a pleasant change from rice and oatmeal! Any recipe with seeds should only be given to babies 8 months and older. Younger babies may have difficulty swallowing the seeds.

Yummy Vanilla Yogurt

2 SERVINGS

1 cup plain whole-fat yogurt, homemade or
    commercial
½ teaspoon vanilla extract
2 tablespoons sugar

1. Place yogurt in bowl.
2. Stir in vanilla and sugar. Mix until smooth.
3. Use immediately, or refrigerate extra and use
   within 2–3 days.

Make it Sweeter

Commercial or homemade plain yogurt can be made
sweeter and tastier for your baby with a few simple
additions. Try your baby on plain yogurt first, but if
he seems not to like the sour taste, try this sweeter
version.

Yes Please, Yogurt Popsicles

8 SERVINGS

1 cup plain whole-fat yogurt, homemade or
*   commercial*
1 rack of popsicle molds

1. Stir the yogurt well.
2. Pour into clean popsicle molds, about ¾ of the
   way full
3. Place in the freezer and let freeze overnight.

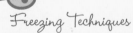

Freezing Techniques

If your popsicles aren't freezing well, try not putting
them in the freezer door—opening and closing the
door frequently will prevent an even freeze. Make sure
the freezer isn't overcrowded, because that will prevent the cold air from circulating. Also, freeze yogurt
popsicles immediately after preparing them.

Homemade Carrot Apple Juice

YIELDS 12 OUNCES

1 pound fresh carrots
½ cup prepared or homemade apple juice

1. Wash and scrub the carrots. Cut off both ends.
2. Push the carrots through a juicing machine, following the manufacturer's instructions. Catch the juice in a clean cup.
3. Mix in the apple juice, and stir thoroughly.
4. Refrigerate the leftovers, and use within 1–2 days.

Juice

Carrot juice is loaded with antioxidants, so it's a very healthy drink for your baby. For variety, try mixing in ½ cup pear juice. Other tasty flavors you could make include carrot peach juice or carrot grape juice.

Homemade Amazing Apple Juice

YIELDS ½ CUP

2 fresh apples
⅛ teaspoon of ascorbic acid (vitamin C)

1. Wash each apple well, and cut in half. Remove the peel, core, and seeds.
2. Run the apples through either an apple press or a juicer.
3. Pour the juice through a fine-mesh cheesecloth to remove any chunks.
4. Measure the juice you've produced. To keep it from turning brown and gathering sediment, add powdered ascorbic acid (vitamin C), in the proportion of .1 ounce of powder to 20 cups of juice. For ½ cup of juice, you'd only need to add about ⅛ teaspoon of vitamin C.
5. Refrigerate immediately, and use within 1–2 days. If you want the juice to last longer (without turning into vinegar) you'll need to pasteurize it.

Do-It-Yourself Pops

When baby's not feeling well, one of the most important things you can do for her is keep her hydrated. If she refuses to take an electrolyte drink from a bottle, try freezing it in ice-cube trays. Slide half of a popsicle stick into each cube once partially frozen so you have a convenient handle to use later.

Great Homemade Grape Juice

YIELDS 1–2 CUPS

2 cup grapes
6 cups water

1. Wash the grapes thoroughly, removing any stems or blemished fruit. Mash them with a spoon or potato masher until you start to see the juice running out.
2. Place in a saucepan with the water. Bring to a boil, then simmer for 10–15 minutes. When cooked, strain the grapes and mash again.
3. Prepare another saucepan by draping 2 layers of cheesecloth over it. Secure the cloth to the pot with tape.
4. Pour the strained grapes over the cheesecloth, then allow to sit for about 12 hours (or overnight) in the refrigerator.
5. In the morning, discard the leftover fruit and cheesecloth. Run the juice through a fine-mesh strainer to remove any chunks. Refrigerate immediately, and use within 1–2 days.

Some Like It Pulpy!

If you're making homemade juice to serve to a young baby, it's better to filter out all the pulp and chunky bits. For older children or grownups, though, feel free to add some of the fruit back in.

Homemade Soy Milk

10 SERVINGS

½ cup dry soybeans   2 cups water

1. Rinse and drain the soybeans several times in cold water. Place in a pot, cover with water, and soak overnight in the refrigerator.
2. Put the beans in a food processor with about 1½ cups water. Purée until smooth, about 4 minutes.
3. Bring 4 tablespoons of water to a boil. Add soybean purée and stir constantly until the mixture starts to foam.
4. Pour the hot purée into a pressing bag or very fine colander. Extrude the soy milk through the holes into a pot. When done, heat the pot to boiling and cook for 6–7 minutes, stirring constantly.
5. Remove milk from heat, and store in a sealed container in refrigerator.

It's All in the Taste

While many "big people" like the taste of plain, unadulterated soy milk, children may balk because it doesn't have the richness of dairy milk, or the sweetness of fruit juice. Try adding a little sugar or artificial sweetener while the soy milk is still warm, stirring until it is completely dissolved, then chill. Be sure to shake or stir well before serving.

Silken Tofu Cubes

1 SERVING

1 2-inch-square piece of tofu

1. Place the tofu on a plate.
2. Slice into small cubes, about ½-inch pieces.
3. Allow baby to pick up the tofu and self-feed, under careful supervision to prevent choking.

Chinese Versus Japanese Tofu

There are two basic types of easily-available tofu: Chinese and Japanese. Chinese tofu comes in extra-firm, firm, and soft. Japanese tofu is the silken variety because of the way it's manufactured, it tends to be creamier and almost custard-like.

The Best Homemade Bagels

12 SERVINGS

1 package active dry yeast
4 cups all-purpose flour
4 tablespoons sugar
1½ tablespoons sugar
8 cups water
2 tablespoons oil
1 teaspoon salt, optional

1. Preheat oven to 375°F. Pour the yeast, 1 table-spoon of flour and 1 tablespoon sugar into a bowl along with 1 cup of warm water. Mix until dissolved, then allow it to sit for 10–15 minutes, or until the yeast forms a sponge.
2. Add in the rest of the flour, sugar, oil, and salt. Mix, adding flour if needed, until the dough is stiff. Cover and let the dough rise for about

Bagels

Bagels are the ultimate teething food: chewy enough to feel good on baby's tender gums, nutritious, and big enough that baby can't shove the whole thing in her mouth at once. Experiment with adding sesame or poppy seeds for other members of the family.

15 minutes. While the dough is rising, fill a large saucepan with water and bring to a boil.

3. Split the dough into 12 balls. Poke a hole in each ball and round it out so that the hole stretches to about a 1-inch diameter. Drop into the boiling water in batches of 3. Boil 2 minutes on each side, using tongs to flip bagel over.

4. As each bagel comes out of the boiling pot, drain briefly on paper towels. Place the bagels on a greased baking sheet, then bake for 20–25 minutes.

5. Allow bagels to cool completely. Supervise closely to make sure your baby doesn't bite off a large piece.

Chapter 4

Lay the Groundwork

WHEN IT COMES TO menu planning, variety is important for more than making toddler taste buds tingle. No single food is perfect, so children need to eat many different foods for optimal nutrition. Only a few generalities are certain: fresh foods are better than processed; pesticide-free food is healthier. So take up cooking and, if you can, go organic!

12–18 Months

The following recipes are fresh and interesting variations of familiar sounding meals—specially modified to fit your growing one-year-old's needs. From eggs, to pasta, to fish, toddlers will surely enjoy these new taste sensations.

Apricot Rice, Just Right

2 SERVINGS

¼ cup brown rice
½ cup water
1 ripe apricot

1. Combine the rice with ½ cup water in a saucepan. Bring to a boil, then simmer for 20 minutes, or until all liquid has been absorbed.
2. Wash the apricot well. Peel it, remove the pit, and chop into small pieces.
3. Combine the rice and apricot in a food processor or blender. Pulse to desired consistency.
4. If making a thin mixture, purée until smooth. Add breastmilk or formula as needed to make the mixture creamier.

Out of Season Apricots

If apricots aren't in season, feel free to substitute canned apricots. Just try to find ones that aren't canned in heavy syrup, because that will add a lot of unwanted sugar or corn syrup to the dish. Look for fruit canned in natural juices only, or at least in light syrup. If not, use peaches, nectarines, or another stone fruit—baby will never know the difference.

Corn Cereal Creation

2 SERVINGS

¼ cup ground corn
1 cup water

1. Pour the water into a small saucepan. Bring to a rolling boil.
2. Add the finely ground corn into the boiling water, stirring constantly for about 1 minute.
3. Cover the pot, turn down the heat to low and simmer for 8–10 minutes, or until the corn turns into a thick cereal. Stir occasionally to prevent sticking and burning.
4. If the corn cereal is too thick for baby, thin it out with a bit of breastmilk or formula.

Cornmeal

Corn is a common allergen, so it shouldn't be introduced until baby's first birthday. From that point on, you can experiment with different kinds of ground corn. Cornmeal is readily available, for example, but corn cones (another type of ground corn) are usually more finely ground. Use the most finely ground corn you can find.

Lovely Rice-Lentil Cereal

3 SERVINGS

¼ cup white rice
⅛ cup lentils
⅛ cup chopped tomatoes
1 cup water

1. Combine the lentils in a saucepan with the water. Bring to a boil, then cook at a rapid boil for 15 minutes.
2. Add the rice and tomatoes, then reduce to a simmer. Cook for another 25–30 minutes, or until all liquid is absorbed.
3. Once cool, fork-mash or purée the meal according to baby's preference. Thin with water, breastmilk, or formula if desired.

Lentils and Tomatoes

Lentils and tomatoes go well together because the slightly acidic nature of the tomato balances the thick flavor of the beans. Just be sure that baby hasn't shown any sign of allergy to tomatoes.

Baby Muesli

2 SERVINGS

¼ cup regular oats (not quick-cooking)
1 ripe pear
2 ripe apricots
½ ripe banana
1 cup milk (or soy milk)

1. Peel the banana, pear, and apricots. Remove all stems, seeds, and pits. Chop into small pieces.
2. Pour the oats and milk into a saucepan. Bring to a boil, then cook at a boil for about 30 seconds.
3. Add in the fruit pieces and stir thoroughly.
4. Cover the pot, turn down the heat to low, and simmer for 8–10 minutes, or until the oats are smooth and thick. Stir occasionally to prevent sticking and burning.
5. Depending on baby's preference, either serve as-is, or purée in a food processor for a creamier texture.

Muesli Versus Granola

Muesli is traditionally made of uncooked oats, though for babies you should cook the oats first. For older children or adults, however, you can make muesli by mixing uncooked oats with dried fruits and serving with milk. Granola, while still made primarily from oats, is usually baked with honey or other sweeteners to give it a sweet, crunchy taste.

Kiwi Protein Power Food

1 SERVING

1 ripe kiwi fruit
½ ripe banana
¼ cup cottage cheese

1. Trim the ends of the kiwi. Ease a spoon under the peel, going all the way around the fruit, until the fleshy center slides out. Cut into small pieces.
2. Peel the banana, removing any brown spots.
3. Combine the fruits on a plate. Add the cottage cheese, and fork-mash to desired consistency.
4. If the mixture has too much texture for baby, add a little yogurt and continue fork-mashing until creamy.

Kiwi

Kiwi livens up any dish because of its vibrant green color and sweet flavor. It's also high in fiber, especially if baby eats the seeds along with the fleshy fruit. To tell when a kiwi is ripe, squeeze it lightly. It'll give under pressure but won't fall apart.

Dynamic Duo: Bananas and OJ

1 SERVING

1 ripe banana
1 medium juice orange

1. Slice the orange in half. Juice it using either a juicing machine or a manual juicer. You can also simply squeeze firmly over a bowl. Strain out any pulp or seeds.
2. Peel the banana, removing any brown spots. Cut into slices and place on a plate.
3. Fork-mash the banana, slowly adding in the orange juice. Continue mashing until the texture is such that baby can eat it with a spoon.

Too Soupy!

Add too much liquid to a puréed fruit meal? If baby is older than a year, try adding a bit of yogurt (soy or milk) to thicken it up. Or, if you have a bit of leftover baby rice or baby oatmeal, mix that in—it makes a great instant thickener.

Minted Bananas and Strawberries

4 SERVINGS

1 *pint fresh strawberries*
1 *large banana*
10 *large fresh mint leaves*

1. Rinse strawberries and remove hulls (leaves and central core) with a sharp knife. Cut into pieces.
2. Peel banana, removing any brown spots. Cut into pieces.
3. With a sharp knife, cut the mint leaves into thin strips.
4. Place all ingredients in steamer basket. Place in pot over about 2 inches of water. Bring to a boil, and steam for about 5 minutes.
5. Serve in pieces, or mash to desired consistency.

Which Mint?

Mint leaves are a great ingredient to add a refreshing taste to everything from lemonade to fruit. You can easily grow mint yourself in your garden or in a pot, or buy fresh leaves at the store in the fresh herb section. If you grow mint yourself, you can choose from peppermint, spearmint, and other varieties.

Great Steamed Grapes and Squash

5 SERVINGS

1 medium butternut squash
15–20 large, seedless green grapes

1. Wash squash. Peel, remove seeds, and cut into 1-inch cubes.
2. Place squash in a steamer basket. Place in pot over about 2 inches of water. Bring to a boil and steam for about 6 minutes.
3. Wash the grapes. Cut in half, if desired.
4. Add grapes to steamer basket and steam for another 6 minutes, or until tender when pricked with a fork.
5. Serve in pieces, or mash to desired consistency.

Grapes

Have you ever tried cooking grapes? They add a great taste when paired with butternut squash. Steaming grapes makes them more tender and less of a choking hazard. In addition, you don't need to peel them. You should still supervise your child closely when eating any kind of grapes.

Terrific Trio:
Bananas with Papaya and Mango

5 SERVINGS

1 small ripe papaya
1 large ripe mango
2 ripe bananas

1. Slice papaya in half and remove seeds and skin. Cut into small chunks.
2. Remove skin and pit from mango, and cut into small chunks.
3. Peel bananas and cut into slices.
4. Place papaya in a steamer basket, and steam for about 5 minutes. Add mango and banana, and steam for another 5 minutes, or until very tender.
5. Serve in pieces, or mash to desired consistency.

Mango Tips

It's almost impossible to eat a mango without making a huge mess. One tip is to slice both "cheeks" off the mango—cut off the rounded parts on both sides of the pit. Then with a sharp knife, cut squares in the flesh while still on the skin, push the skin inside out, and slice off the squares. Then dice what's left of the mango off the pit.

Artichoke Leaves, a Fun Finger Food

2 SERVINGS

1 artichoke

1. With sharp knife, cut off artichoke stem near base.
2. Using kitchen scissors, cut the thorn off each artichoke leaf. Cut each leaf about ½ inch down from the tip. Slice across the central core to cut off the tips of the leaves in the central portion.
3. Place artichoke in steamer basket over about 3 inches of water. Steam for 35–40 minutes, or until the bottom leaves can be easily removed.
4. To eat, remove one leaf at a time. Pull leaf between your teeth, scraping the tender flesh off with your bottom teeth. Watch toddlers at all times to make sure they are only eating the bottom of each leaf—discard the rest.
5. When you've eaten all the leaves, use a knife to scrape the "choke," the fuzzy part, off the artichoke heart (the tender middle portion). Eat the heart.

Artichoke Trivia

Artichokes are members of the thistle family, which may explain the thorns and the fuzzy choke in the middle. Artichokes also have a unique characteristic—they contain natural chemicals that make everything you eat immediately afterwards taste sweet! This is yet another reason for toddlers with a sweet tooth to try artichokes.

Clever Cottage Cheese and Cooked Fruit

2 SERVINGS

½ cup cottage cheese
½ peach
4 strawberries
¼ cup water

1. Peel peach, remove pit, and cut into pieces.
2. Remove hull and stem from strawberries and cut into quarters.
3. Place strawberries and peaches in microwave-safe glass dish. Add water and cover loosely with lid or with microwave-safe saran wrap.
4. Microwave on high for 2 minutes. Remove cover carefully and stir. If fruit is not soft, re-cover and heat until soft, 30 seconds at a time. Let cooked fruit cool to lukewarm.
5. Place cottage cheese in bowl. Pour cooked strawberries and peaches on top, including juices.

All About Cottage Cheese

Cottage cheese comes in many varieties—small curd, large curd, low-fat, low-salt, and others. For babies and young children, choose the higher fat varieties. Cottage cheese has a fair amount of salt in it, but avoid the low-sodium types—salt is necessary for the curdling process that makes cottage cheese, so the low-salt varieties tend not to taste very good.

Lovely Lima Beans

2 SERVINGS

¼ cup lima beans (fresh or frozen)
2 cups water or chicken stock

1. Rinse the lima beans.
2. Bring the water or chicken stock to a boil. Add lima beans.
3. Reduce heat and simmer for 25–30 minutes, or until beans are completely tender.
4. Fork-mash to desired consistency, or serve as finger food.

Bean Me Up Scotty

Lima beans, also called butter beans, are a great source of fiber. They have a sweet taste that many babies like right away. To counteract the fiber, though, be sure to offer in small amounts, or combine with a binding fruit such as bananas.

Scrumptious Scrambled Eggs with Cheese

1 SERVING

1 egg
1 tablespoon milk (regular or soy)
2 tablespoons grated cheese

1. Crack the egg into a bowl and add milk. Beat thoroughly.
2. Pour the egg into a medium-hot non-stick frying pan, adding a bit of oil or butter if the egg starts to stick.
3. Scramble the egg, adding the cheese about half-way through. Continue scrambling until egg is cooked and cheese melted.

Cooking with Milk

It's safe to cook with milk as long as you're using pasteurized milk. It's safe to scald milk (heat to just below the boiling point), but you don't want to actually boil it—boiling causes a skin-like layer to form on the surface. Always make sure your milk tastes and smells fresh before serving to baby.

Cream Cheese Tortilla Rollups

1 SERVING

1 tortilla
1 tablespoon cream cheese
1 thin slice of cheese

1. Lay the tortilla out on a microwaveable plate.
2. Spread a thin layer of cream cheese over the tortilla.
3. Lay a thin slice of cheese (American, Swiss, or any other hard cheese that your baby likes) in the middle of the tortilla.
4. Roll up and warm in the microwave for about 10–15 seconds.
5. Cut into small slices and serve as finger food.

Tortillas

You can use either flour or corn tortillas for this recipe. Use corn as long as baby shows no allergy to corn, or flour if baby doesn't have a wheat allergy. Flour tortillas are slightly higher in calories and fat, but may roll up more easily.

Clever Carrot Omelet

1 SERVING

1 egg
1 small carrot
1 tablespoon milk or water
½ tablespoon butter or margarine

1. Wash and peel the carrot. Grate approximately 2 tablespoons.
2. Crack the egg into a bowl and add milk or water. Beat thoroughly.
3. Add grated carrot and stir completely.
4. Melt the butter or margarine in a non-stick frying pan. Pour in the egg mixture and tilt the pan to spread evenly.
5. When the egg is set, flip to cook the other side. When egg is cooked through, remove from heat.
6. Cool to lukewarm, and cut into pieces to serve as finger food or to be eaten with a baby-safe fork.

Grate or Dice?

Finally baby is starting to eat some of the same foods that the grownups do! But not quite. For recipes like omelets that contain vegetables, always grate the veggies rather than dice them. Most new eaters are prone to choking, and baby's already got a lot to deal with when she first tackles the texture of an omelet. Help her out by finely grating the vegetables.

Fantastic Veggie Frittata

3 SERVINGS

½ small zucchini
½ medium carrot
1 small onion
2 eggs
3 cups water

¼ cup milk
¼ cup grated cheese
1 tablespoon butter
or oil

1. Preheat the oven to 350°F.
2. Remove the peel from the onion and carrot. Wash and grate the zucchini, onion, and carrots, about ¼ cup of each. Melt the butter in a saucepan, and sauté the vegetables for 8–10 minutes, or until completely softened.
3. Crack the eggs into a small bowl. Whisk together with the milk and cheese, and mix in vegetables.
4. Place the eggs and vegetables into a greased baking pan. Bake for 35–40 minutes, or until the eggs are completely cooked.
5. Once cool, serve to baby in small pieces or fork-mash to desired consistency.

Make It Crunchy

Dress up this recipe with a crunchy topping, if baby's developmentally ready for it. You can make your own bread crumbs by toasting whole wheat bread, then running it through a food processor or blender. Sprinkle bread crumbs over the frittata, dribble a bit of melted butter on top, and bake.

Simple and Super French Toast

3 SERVINGS

1 egg
3 slices whole-wheat bread
1 tablespoon milk or water
1 tablespoon oil
1 teaspoon white sugar
pinch of cinnamon

1. Combine the egg, milk, sugar, and cinnamon in a medium bowl. Beat thoroughly.
2. Heat oil in a large frying pan. One at a time, dip the bread slices into the egg mixture and soak for about 10 seconds. Flip the bread over and soak on the other side.
3. Place each of the bread slices into the heated pan.
4. Fry on each side until lightly browned, usually 1–3 minutes per side.
5. Let cool completely before cutting into pieces and serving as finger food.

Dress It Up!
Once your baby has mastered simple French toast, try adding fruit to make it a bit more appealing to the rest of the family. Mix a few mashed blueberries or strawberries into the egg mixture, for example. Or, if you want to try a creamier French toast, add a little applesauce into the egg mixture. You can also add a little vanilla or almond extract.

Delightful Duo:
Mashed Avocado and Cottage Cheese

1 SERVING

1 ripe avocado
½ cup cottage cheese

1. Cut a small slice of avocado and remove the peel. Fork-mash on a plate.
2. Combine with the cottage cheese and continue fork-mashing until the mixture is at the desired consistency.
3. If the mix is still too chunky, try fork-mashing in some yogurt, breastmilk, or formula.

Cottage Cheese Please

Cottage cheese is a relative of pot cheese or farmer's cheese; these varieties are basically cottage cheese, which has been pressed. They are very similar to Queso Blanco, a white cheese that is produced by pressing the whey out of cottage cheese. As baby gets older, introduce more variety into her diet by experimenting with these other types of cottage cheese.

Fruity Cream Sauce

2 SERVINGS

½ cup heavy cream
2 tablespoons sugar
½ cup sour cream
½ cup yogurt
4 strawberries or ¼ cup blueberries

1. Pour the cream into a medium metal bowl. Using an egg beater or electric mixer, whip until soft peaks are formed.
2. Fold in the sour cream, yogurt, and sugar until completely mixed.
3. Refrigerate until ready for use.
4. Serve to baby over a small dish of washed and chopped strawberries, blueberries, or other soft fruit.

Fruity Cream

There are several approaches to Fruity Cream. This recipe is for a cream sauce that can be spread over soft fruit. Another method is to purée your fruit first, add equal amounts of water and sugar, mix well with a small amount of cream, and freeze.

Cottage Cheese and Pea Creation

1 SERVING

¼ cup peas (fresh or frozen)
1 cup water
½ cup cottage cheese

1. Wash the peas and place in a saucepan with water. Bring to a boil, then simmer for about 10 minutes, or until peas are very tender.
2. Allow peas to cool, then combine on a plate with the cottage cheese.
3. Fork-mash to desired consistency, or let baby pick up individual peas and pieces of large-curd cottage cheese by himself.

Cheese 'n Peas

If baby is already gumming down cottage cheese and peas separately, this is one of the easiest recipes you can make! Quick to make and entirely healthy, baby can feel good about feeding himself. Mom will feel great about getting a rest while baby self-feeds (or, in some cases, feeds the floor).

Homemade Egg-cellent Pasta

8 SERVINGS

½ pound of flour   2 eggs
pinch of salt

1. Mix the flour and salt together and put the flour in a pile on a clean surface. Use your fingers to make a well in the middle of the flour pile.
2. Crack the eggs into the well and mix with a fork, gradually pulling in flour from the well. When your dough begins to come together, knead for 10–12 minutes, or until you have a smooth dough. Add a teaspoon of water only if necessary.
3. Flour your work surface and roll out the dough until it becomes a nearly transparent sheet. Flip and reflour the surface as necessary.
4. Slice into strands if making spaghetti and cut into squares if using for ravioli or other shaped pasta.
5. Bring a large pot of water to a boil and cook for 4–5 minutes, or until pasta floats to the top of the pot (shorter cooking time than store-bought pasta).

Pasta

Get out the elbow grease for making your own pasta! Store-bought pastas are generally enriched with a variety of minerals and vitamins. However, if you want your baby to have only fresh pasta with no additives, making it yourself is the way to go.

Healthy Whole-Wheat Pasta

1 SERVING

¼ cup Homemade Egg Pasta (page 122) or boxed
spaghetti or other pasta
4 cups of water

1. Bring the water to a rapid boil in a large saucepan.
2. Add pasta and stir to separate the noodles. Continue boiling for 10–15 minutes, or according to package directions. Pasta should be soft and completely cooked.
3. Let cool completely, then cut into ½-inch long pieces for baby to pick up and self-feed.

Cook It Well

While you may prefer your pasta al dente, under-cooked noodles tend to cause young babies to choke. She's not after the perfect sauce or perfect noodle, she just wants something she can mash easily with her gums. Taste pasta before serving and err on the side of overcooking when it comes to pasta.

Noodles with Cheese Please!

3 SERVINGS

¾ cup elbow macaroni (or other shape)
4 cups water
2 tablespoons butter
2 tablespoons all-purpose flour
1½ cups milk
¾ cup grated cheese

1. Bring the water to a rapid boil in a large saucepan.
2. Add the macaroni, stirring to break up the pasta. Cook for 12–15 minutes, or until noodles are completely tender. Drain.
3. In a small saucepan, melt the butter over low heat. Stir in the flour, whisking constantly until it's dissolved. Add milk and cheese, stirring constantly, until it thickens into a sauce.
4. Pour the cheese sauce into the noodles, tossing to mix.
5. Allow to cool before serving to your baby.

Choosing a Cheese

For basic macaroni and cheese, try using Cheddar, Colby, or Monterey Jack cheese. Mozzarella melts very well on pizza, but isn't great for cooking into a baby's meal because it tends to congeal rapidly. Experiment with different kinds of cheeses to see which kind your baby likes the best!

Egg Noodles Plus Peas

¼ cup egg noodles
4 cups of water
2 tablespoons peas

1. Bring the water to a rapid boil in a large saucepan.
2. Add pasta and peas. Stir to separate the noodles.
3. Continue boiling for 10–12 minutes, or according to package directions. Pasta should be soft and completely cooked.
4. Drain the pasta and peas, allowing to cool completely.
5. Cut the noodles into ½-inch long pieces for baby to pick up and self-feed. Can be served with a tablespoon of grated cheese.

Egg Noodles

Egg noodles are typically firmer than regular pasta. They're usually in the form of flat, wide noodles and are great for baking into casseroles. They hold up well with peas, and served together they provide a nice texture complement.

Creamy Coconut Lentils

3 SERVINGS

½ cup lentils
1 teaspoon curry powder
1 cup water
¼ small onion, diced
3 tablespoons coconut, shredded
¼ cup milk (regular or soy)

1. Bring the water to a rapid boil in a medium saucepan.
2. Add lentils, onions, and coconut, and reduce water to a simmer. Cook for about 45 minutes, or until the lentils are completely soft.
3. Add the milk and curry powder, and cook about another 15 minutes.
4. Allow to cool, then fork-mash before serving.

Coconut Facts

High in potassium and fiber, coconut is a nutritious food that many babies like. According to some research, coconuts also have medicinal value in fighting off infection and fungi, and may even help prevent various diseases. Coconut is high in saturated fat, but okay for babies to have on an occasional basis.

Red Lentil Dhal, for All

3 SERVINGS

½ cup split red lentils
2 cups chicken stock or water
½ teaspoon cumin
¼ small onion, diced
¼ mild green chili, diced
¼ teaspoon ginger
¼ teaspoon garlic

1. Peel garlic and ginger. Push both through a press, or chop finely.
2. Bring the water to a rapid boil in a medium saucepan. Add lentils, onions, ginger, garlic, chili, and cumin, and reduce heat to a simmer.
3. Cook for about 45 minutes, or until the lentils are completely soft.
4. Allow to cool, then fork-mash before serving.

Types of Lentils

There are more than 150 variations of lentils out there. The most commonly available tend to be green, red, and brown lentils. They vary widely from country to country, but lentils are widely available throughout North America. Green lentils are particularly popular and have a mild flavor, which is good for baby!

Simply Sensational Hummus

2 SERVINGS

1 cup canned chickpeas
1 tablespoon tahini
1 teaspoon lemon juice
1 teaspoon olive oil
1 teaspoon cumin
1 tablespoon water
1 clove garlic , optional

1. If using garlic, peel.
2. Rinse the precooked chickpeas. Place in food processor or blender and purée completely. Add the garlic and purée until well chopped and smooth.
3. Add the olive oil, tahini, cumin, and lemon juice. Continue puréeing for about a minute, scraping down the sides of the bowl as necessary.
4. Add enough water to make a smooth paste. Purée until smooth.

Tahini

Tahini is a Middle Eastern sesame seed paste. You can find it in a can in the international or Middle-Eastern food section of your grocery store. You can make tahini sauce by mixing equal amounts of water and tahini paste with a little lemon juice. This dipping sauce is tasty for falafel, vegetables, and other foods.

Baby Ratatouille

4 SERVINGS

1 *small zucchini, diced*
½ *small onion, diced*
½ *small eggplant, diced*
16-*ounce can stewed tomatoes*
½ *teaspoon oregano*
½ *teaspoon parsley*
½ *teaspoon basil*
1 *tablespoon olive oil*

1. Heat the oil in a medium saucepan. Sauté onion until it begins to brown and turns translucent.
2. Add the eggplant, zucchini, and tomatoes into the saucepan. Bring to a boil, then reduce to a simmer.
3. Cook for 20 minutes. Stir in the herbs, then cook for another 20 minutes. Allow to cool, then fork-mash before serving.

Ratatouille

Ratatouille is a French vegetable stew. As shown here, this recipe can be cooked on the stove, but it's also a fantastic slow cooker meal. Microwaving is also acceptable, although the vegetables won't have the chance to simmer together and the flavors will not be as developed.

Terrific Trio:
Broccoli with Oranges and Almonds

3 SERVINGS

½ head of broccoli   2 tablespoons butter
¼ cup sliced almonds   4 cups water
½ orange

1. Wash the broccoli and remove the stem. Dice into small florets.
2. Heat butter in a medium saucepan. Toast the almonds for about 5 minutes, or until lightly browned.
3. Bring water to a boil. Add broccoli and cook for about 15 minutes, or until broccoli is tender.
4. Slice the orange in half and remove the fruit with a grapefruit spoon. Cut into small pieces. Toss cooked broccoli, almonds, and oranges together.
5. If the textures are too challenging, omit the almonds and purée the broccoli and orange, adding breastmilk or formula as necessary to thin the mixture.

Vegetables with Fruit
A great way to serve vegetables: mix them with sweet fruit! Even fussy eaters will find something they like in this broccoli dish, which combines fruit with broccoli and nuts.

Lentils They'll Love,
with Butternut Squash

3 SERVINGS

1 small bell pepper
½ butternut squash
½ cup lentils
½ teaspoon cinnamon

4 cups water
2 tablespoons orange
   juice

1. Rinse the lentils and place in a pot with the water. Bring to a boil.
2. Wash the pepper and remove the seeds. Dice into small pieces and add to lentils.
3. Wash the squash and slice in half. Peel the squash and remove the seeds. Dice into pieces, and add to the lentils.
4. Add the cinnamon and continue cooking for 40 minutes, or until lentils are completely tender.
5. Allow to cool, then fork-mash with orange juice before serving.

Butternut Squash

The richness of squash in this recipe combines well with the savory bell pepper and the protein-filled lentils. Children will like the sweetness from the squash and the orange juice.

Broccoli and Cornmeal, Good Company

2 SERVINGS

¼ cup cornmeal
½ small head broccoli
3 cups water

1. Wash the broccoli and remove all stems. Cut into small florets.
2. Bring 2 cups of water to a boil. Add the broccoli into a steamer basket, then cook for about 15 minutes or until broccoli is tender.
3. In another saucepan, bring ¾ cup water to a boil. Slowly add the cornmeal, stirring constantly until it is dissolved. Reduce the heat and simmer for about 15 minutes, or according to the directions on the package.
4. When the cornmeal is finished, drain the broccoli and mix it in with the cornmeal.
5. Allow to cool, then fork-mash before serving.

Yellow or White Cornmeal?

For the purposes of making food for your baby, it doesn't really matter which type of cornmeal you choose. Yellow corn has a buttery taste, while white corn tends to be sweeter. Either way, baby will get the nutrition she needs.

Baby's First Rice and Beans

4 SERVINGS

1 cup red beans
½ cup white rice
6 cups water

1. Rinse the beans and place in a large saucepan along with 5 cups of water. Bring to a boil.
2. Reduce heat and simmer until beans are tender, about 2 hours.
3. In another saucepan, pour 1 cup of water and ½ cup of uncooked white rice. Bring to a boil, then reduce the heat and simmer for about 35 minutes, or according to the directions on the package.
4. When the beans are tender, drain and serve on top of rice.
5. Allow to cool, then fork-mash before serving, or serve as finger food.

A Perfect Match

Rice and beans are a staple food in many parts of the world. They go together for a reason: beans provide a protein that's lacking in amino acids, but it's rounded out by serving it along with nuts or grains, like rice, to make a filling, complete protein.

Potato Pumpkin Mash

3 SERVINGS

1 small sweet potato or yam, diced
¼ small cooking pumpkin
1 tablespoon butter or margarine
½ cup shredded cheese
4 cups of water

1. Preheat the oven to 350°F. Slice the pumpkin in quarters, removing any seeds. Remove the skin, and dice the pumpkin flesh into small pieces.
2. Combine the potato and pumpkin in a saucepan with the water. Bring to a boil, then simmer for 30 minutes, or until the vegetables are tender.
3. Place the drained vegetables in an baking dish. Dot with butter and sprinkle the cheese on top.
4. Bake for 15 minutes, or until the cheese is melted. Let cool completely before serving.

Cooking with Pumpkin

Pumpkins are part of the same family as squashes, and both can be cooked and eaten. There are different varieties of pumpkins—the ones you carve on Halloween won't taste particularly good! Look for pumpkins called "cooking pumpkins," "pie pumpkins," or some other designation that indicates that they are meant to be eaten, not carved.

Simply Delicious Steamed Tofu

1 SERVING

1 ounce tofu
2 tablespoons water

1. Place tofu in a glass microwaveable dish, adding a little water in the bottom of the dish. Cover with microwave-safe plastic wrap.
2. Microwave on high for 30 seconds or until warm.

Tofu

Tofu is a great food for baby—it's soft, easy to mash, and high in protein. Bean curd is available in most grocery stores, and is a terrific finger food.

Un-Fancy White Fish

2 SERVINGS

1 small white fish fillet
1 tablespoon olive oil
¼ cup all-purpose flour
dash salt

1. Wash the fish fillet, remove all bones, and sprinkle lightly with salt.
2. Dredge the fillet in flour. Shake to remove any excess.
3. Heat the oil in a frying pan. Fry the fillet until brown, 4–5 minutes.
4. Flip and cook on the other side 4–5 minutes, or until fish is cooked through and flakes with a fork.
5. Allow to cool, then fork-mash before serving.

Allergy Alert

Experts recommend holding off on seafood until baby is 3 years old. Seafood is a common allergen and shellfish allergies can be quite severe. If baby has shown no sign of allergies (or eczema), fish is safe after the first year, but hold off until later on foods like shrimp and crab.

First Timer's Fish and Vegetables

3 SERVINGS

1 small white fish fillet
½ small zucchini
½ medium carrot
⅛ teaspoon lemon juice
½ tablespoon butter

1. Preheat the oven to 375°F. Wash and peel the carrot. Wash the zucchini, then cut both into thin slices.
2. Wash the fish fillet, removing all bones.
3. Prepare a double-layer of aluminum foil about 18-inches square, and lightly grease the inside of the foil.
4. Place the fish and vegetables in the foil, dot the top with butter, then seal the packet and place in a baking dish. Bake for 45 minutes, or until the fish is opaque and flakes easily.
5. Allow to cool, then fork-mash before serving.

Oven-Baked

Oven-baked fish is a healthy meal for baby, and can be a time-saver as well. Prepare this meal, pop it in the oven and, an hour later, dinner is served! Veggies will bake faster when sliced thinly, so go for thin coins rather than chunks in this recipe.

Hawaiian Poached Pork Plate

2 SERVINGS

¼ cup ground pork (about 1–2 ounces)
¼ cup pineapple
¼ cup green pepper, diced
1 cup water

1. Cut up the pineapple into small chunks.
2. Bring the water to a boil in a medium saucepan. Add pork. Simmer for 15–20 minutes or until pork is completely cooked.
3. Drain pork and return to saucepan. Add pineapple and green pepper, and continue simmering for 10 minutes, or until vegetables are heated through and soft.
4. Allow to cool, then fork-mash or purée before serving.

Canned Is Okay

If fresh pineapples aren't available, canned pineapple is perfectly acceptable for this recipe. As long as you get the variety that's not made with heavy syrup, canned pineapple may even be preferable because you can also use the juice instead of water to provide additional flavor to the pork while it's cooking.

Never Fail Fish Chowder with Corn

2 SERVINGS

1 small white fish fillet
⅛ cup corn
⅛ cup peas
1 tablespoon butter

½ medium white
potato, diced
¼ cup milk
2 cups water

1. Combine potato, corn, and peas in a saucepan with 2 cups of water. Bring to a boil, then cook for 25 minutes, or until the potatoes are soft.
2. Wash the fish fillet, removing all bones. Place fish into the bottom of a microwave-safe dish and add enough water to cover the bottom of the dish. Cover with either a lid or microwave-safe plastic wrap.
3. Cook fish in the microwave on high for 3 minutes. Let rest, then cook for another 3–4 minutes. Fish is done when it flakes easily with a fork.
4. Drain the vegetables. Add the fish, butter, and milk, stirring over low heat until the chowder thickens. Allow to cool, then fork-mash or puree before serving.

The Origins of Chowder

According to most sources, the soup we know as chowder originated in England in the 1700s. Fishermen would start a pot of water boiling in the morning and, as the day wore on, would add fresh fish, vegetables, bread, and any other available ingredients. By day's end, a thick soup was ready for all.

Fruity Chicken Casserole

3 SERVINGS

½ half chicken breast (about 4 ounces)
1 small apple
½ orange
2 tablespoons apple juice
2 tablespoons orange juice

1. Preheat the oven to 350°F. Wash and peel the apple. Remove the core and seeds, then dice the fruit into small pieces. Place in a greased baking dish.
2. Wash the chicken breast, then place on top of the apples.
3. Mix the orange and apple juice together and pour over the chicken.
4. Bake for 45 minutes, or until chicken juices run clear.
5. Allow to cool, then fork-mash or purée before serving.

Easy on the Tummy

Many "grown-up" chicken casseroles are made with heavy cream and canned soups. For young babies, it's best to know exactly what you're cooking with, down to the last ingredient. Try this lighter, fruity variation on the chicken casserole instead.

Baby's First Birthday Cake

8 SERVINGS

3 cups flour
1½ cups sugar
½ teaspoon salt
1 teaspoon vanilla
    extract

¾ cup butter or mar-
    garine, softened
1 tablespoon baking
    powder
5 egg yolks

1. Preheat the oven to 350°F. Grease three 8-inch round cake pans, line the bottoms with waxed paper, and grease and flour the pans.
2. Cream the butter with 1 cup of sugar. When mixed, add flour, salt, and baking powder.
3. Beat in eggs yolks, one at a time. Add vanilla and last ½ cup sugar.
4. Fill each cake pan about halfway, then bake for 20–25 minutes or until a toothpick inserted into the center comes out clean.
5. Cool in the pans for 10 minutes, then remove onto wire racks and let the cakes cool completely.

Quick Cake Frosting

For a triple layer cake, beat ½ cup of butter with an electric mixer. Once the butter is fluffy, gradually add 3 cups of confectioners' sugar and 3 tablespoons of milk or water. Continue mixing until the frosting is a spreadable consistency. If it's too runny, add more sugar; if it's too stiff to spread, just add more liquid.

First-Rate Rice Pudding

3 SERVINGS

½ cup white rice
1¼ cup milk (regular or soy)
2 teaspoons white or brown sugar
¼ teaspoon vanilla extract

1. Bring 1 cup of milk and rice to a scalding point (watch carefully so the milk doesn't boil).
2. Reduce to a simmer, then cook for 30 minutes, or according to package directions. Rice is done when the liquid is absorbed and rice is fluffy.
3. Give the rice a good stir. Add sugar, vanilla, and ¼ cup milk.
4. Simmer over low heat for about 10 minutes, or until the liquid is mostly absorbed.
5. Allow to cool, then fork-mash or purée before serving.

Rice Pudding

Looking for a way to use up that leftover rice? Rice pudding is an excellent choice. This method yields a boiled rice pudding, which involves making your own rice; if you have leftover rice, place it and the other ingredients in a baking dish, then bake at 350°F for 45 minutes.

Baby's First Apple Pie

2 SERVINGS

1 red apple	1/8 teaspoon cinnamon
1 teaspoon brown sugar	1/8 cup rice powder
1/8 teaspoon lemon juice	2 cups water

1. Wash, peel, core, and chop the apple.
2. Put apple pieces in a small saucepan with 1½ cups of water, lemon juice, sugar, and cinnamon. Bring to a boil, then simmer for 25 minutes, or until apple is very soft. Stir occasionally.
3. In another small saucepan, bring ½ cup water to a boil. Add the rice powder and stir for 30 seconds. Cover the pot, turn down the heat to low, and simmer for 7–8 minutes, or until the rice is a smooth, thick consistency. Stir occasionally.
4. When the apple is cooked, fork-mash. Mix in the cooked rice cereal until it reaches the desired consistency.

Apple Pie

Apple pie for baby is just like apple pie for grown-ups—except without the pie shell! Babies don't need all the shortening or butter in a typical pie crust, and it will often be too chewy for easy gumming. Try this recipe instead, because it'll give your baby all of the flavors of homemade apple pie.

Just Peachy Cobbler

2 SERVINGS

1 fresh peach
1 teaspoon brown sugar
⅛ cup rice powder

⅛ teaspoon cinnamon
2 cups water

1. Preheat oven to 350°F.
2. Wash the peach and cut into thin slices. Remove the skin.
3. Place peach into a small, greased baking dish with brown sugar and cinnamon. Give it a quick stir, then bake for 30 minutes, or until peaches are completely soft.
4. In a small saucepan, bring ½ cup water to a boil. Add the rice powder and stir for 30 seconds. Cover the pot, turn down the heat to low, and simmer for 7–8 minutes, or until the rice is a smooth, thick consistency. Stir occasionally to prevent sticking.
5. When the peach is cooked, fork-mash. Mix in the cooked rice cereal until the cobbler reaches the desired consistency.

Cobbling Together a Dessert

Cobblers are fruit desserts that are traditionally cooked in deep-dish pans. They're historically made with whatever fruits are in season; blueberry, blackberry, apricot, and apple are all popular cobbler flavors. Cobblers are distinguished from other baked fruit desserts because they're usually topped with a sweet biscuit dough.

Lip-Smackable Baked Apples

1 SERVING

1 apple
1 teaspoon white sugar
⅛ teaspoon cinnamon
¼ cup water

1. Preheat the oven to 350°F. Wash the apple. Remove the top core, leaving the apple intact.
2. Sprinkle sugar and cinnamon on the inside of the apple. Pour the water into a small baking dish, then place the apple in the center. Bake at for about 45 minutes, or until apple is completely cooked.
3. When cooled, fork-mash to a suitable consistency. If desired, the entire skin can be removed once the apple is cooked.

Make a Dumpling Out of It

A fun trick for toddlers or older children is, instead of baked fruit, to make baked fruit dumplings! Combine 1 cup flour, ½ cup shortening, 2 tablespoons of ice water, and a dash of salt to make a dough. Knead for a couple of minutes, then wrap around your fruit and seal with a tight pinch. Bake at a slightly higher temperature, around 400°F.

Chapter 5

Keep Up the Hard Work!

THE FIRST AND SECOND times tots taste peas, broccoli, and any number of other foods parents consider healthy, it is common for toddlers to turn up their noses at them. After trying again and again, the best recourse, nutritionists say, is for parents to try yet again. It can take eight to ten exposures before a youngster develops a taste for a new food.

18–24 Months

The following recipes are perfect for your one-and-a-half-year old. The combination of new flavors, colors, and textures will excite your little one and encourage him/her to try new things. The nutritious quality of these meals will surely motivate you too!

Fresh and Fruity Salad

3 SERVINGS

1 kiwi	¼ cup raspberries
¼ cup strawberries	½ small mango
¼ cup blueberries	½ cup seedless grapes

1. Wash the kiwi well and trim off both ends. Slide a tablespoon between the fleshy fruit and the peel. Run the spoon around the entire edge, and the fruit should slide out intact. Cut into small pieces.
2. Wash the berries and remove any stems. Cut the strawberries into quarters. Blueberries and raspberries can either be served whole or, if they're large, cut in half.
3. Remove skin and pit from mango. Slice into small pieces.
4. Wash the grapes and slice each in half.
5. Combine all fruits in a baby-safe bowl, and refrigerate until ready to use. Fork-mash if desired.

Fruit Salad

Fruit salad is one of the true joys of summer. And the best part: you can substitute any of the ingredients with whatever is in season. It's nice to provide a combination of flavors, colors, and textures; just make sure the pieces are the right size for your child to pick up with her fingers.

Island Coconut and Fruit Salad

2 SERVINGS

¼ cup shredded coconut
½ cup pineapple
½ cup mandarin oranges or tangerine
½ cup papaya

1. Dice the pineapple into small chunks.
2. If using canned mandarin oranges, slice each piece in half. If using fresh tangerine, peel and remove seeds, then cut each piece in thirds.
3. Slice papaya in half and remove seeds and skin. Cut into small chunks.
4. Combine the fruits in a baby-safe bowl and mix with the coconut. Refrigerate until ready to use. Fork-mash if desired.

Mandarin Oranges

The mandarin orange is about the size of a tangerine but usually has a redder skin. The Clementine is one of the classes that encompasses mandarin oranges. They are native to Southeast Asia, but are also grown in the warm American Southwest.

Favorite Bread Crumb Peach Pudding

2 SERVINGS

1 cup all-purpose flour
½ cup brown sugar
1 egg
½ cup bread crumbs
1 peach

1 teaspoon light cane
    syrup
¼ teaspoon baking
    soda
¼ cup milk

1. Peel the peach and remove the pit. Dice into small pieces.
2. Combine the flour, sugar, milk, peach, baking soda, and bread crumbs in a bowl. Mix well.
3. Add in the egg and cane syrup. Continue mixing until all ingredients are thoroughly combined.
4. Fill a large pot with several inches of water. Place a steaming rack inside the pot. Place on the stove and bring the water to a boil. Pour the recipe into a pudding steamer and cover. Cook for about 4 hours, or until the pudding is completely set.

Steaming a Pudding

Making an authentic steamed pudding is not an easy task, but it's a skill worth learning if it's something you plan to make on a regular basis. The main pieces of equipment you'll need are a large pot with a steaming rack and a pudding steamer. A pudding steamer is a metal vessel that will fit in side your steaming pot, and the pudding goes inside this pudding steamer.

Make Your Own, Melon Bowls with Yogurt

2 SERVINGS

1 small cantaloupe or honeydew melon
1 cup yogurt
½ cup blueberries

1. Slice the melon in half. Slice a small piece of shell off the bottom so that the melon will sit easily on a plate.
2. Scoop out and discard all seeds.
3. Wash the blueberries well, sort out any damaged berries. If using large berries, cut each in half.
4. Fill the hollow in the melon with yogurt. Top with berries.
5. If baby has trouble scooping the melon out, assist by removing pieces using a melon baller or grapefruit spoon.

Melon

Just about any small melon can be used for this recipe, and it's a fun one for small children to help prepare. Allow your child to scoop out the melon seeds with a spoon or an ice-cream scoop, and encourage her to eat the yogurt directly from the melon. Help start her out on a road to healthy eating!

Carrot Peels for Snacking

1 SERVING

1 carrot

1. Wash and peel the carrot. Trim off both ends.
2. Using a vegetable peeler, peel off thin strips of carrot. Serve as finger food.

Carrots

Carrots are loaded with vitamins A and E, and are great for babies. Carrot peels are soft enough to be gummed with fewer teeth, but have all the nutrition.

Chummy Cucumbers and Dip

1 SERVING

½ cup cucumber
2 tablespoons sour cream
2 tablespoons mayonnaise
dash of salt
dash of dill

1. Wash and peel the cucumber. Cut into thin slices.
2. Mix together the sour cream, mayonnaise, salt, and dill. Serve as a dipping sauce for cucumber slices.

Leftover Cucumber Ideas

Try making a light Japanese salad out of leftover cucumber! Prepare a sauce with ¼ cup rice vinegar, 1 tablespoon sugar, and a dash of salt. Slice the left-over cucumber into thin rings, then place in a dish and pour the sauce on top. It's best served chilled. Be sure to offer your toddler a taste—some children actually like the pungent vinegar.

Funny Bell Pepper Faces

1 SERVING

¼ green pepper
1 cherry tomato
1 slice cheese
1 flour or corn tortilla

½ carrot
1 tablespoon peanut
    butter

1. Place the tortilla on a flat plate. Slice the cherry tomato in half. Place on the tortilla for eyes.
2. Slice the bell pepper in half and remove all seeds. Cut 5–10 thin strips, then place at the top of the tortilla for hair.
3. Cut the cheese into 2 half-circles. Place at the sides of the tortilla for ears.
4. Wash and peel the carrot. Grate several pieces and place on the tortilla for the mouth and eyebrows.
5. When the vegetables are all positioned the way you like them, affix each to the tortilla with a dab of peanut butter.

Peppers

Red, green, or yellow bell peppers are sweet and crunchy. Their hotter cousins, such as the jalapeño or the cayenne, will bring tears to your eyes and do much worse for a toddler. Hot peppers contain capsaicin, an alkaloid that forms the basis of pepper sprays. Good for people who thrive on spicy food, but keep it out of your toddler's meal.

Pea Pods

1 SERVING

½ cup sugar snap pea pods
2 cups water
2 teaspoons butter
⅛ teaspoon oregano
⅛ teaspoon parsley

1. If using fresh pea pods, select ones that are firm, bright-green, and medium-sized. Snap the ends off, and remove the strings from each pea.
2. Bring the water to a boil. Add the peas, then boil for about 8 minutes, or until the shells are tender.
3. Cut each cooked pea in half.
4. Either serve as-is, or prepare a butter herb sauce by melting the butter in a small saucepan and stirring in the herbs. When thoroughly mixed, toss with the peas.

Veggie Dips

Vegetables can be dipped into just about any sauce your child might like. Try an Asian dipping sauce with 2 tablespoons soy sauce and ⅛ teaspoon sesame oil. Add a dash of pepper, garlic powder, and sugar. Or offer a mustard dip: 1 tablespoon mayonnaise, 1 tablespoon sour cream, and 1 teaspoon of mustard.

Parmesan Buttery Noodles

1 SERVING

¼ cup egg noodles
4 cups of water
½ tablespoon butter or margarine
1 tablespoon Parmesan

1. Bring the water to a rapid boil in a large saucepan.
2. While the water is boiling, grate about a tablespoon of parmesan cheese (or substitute pre-grated cheese).
3. Add pasta and stir to separate the noodles. Continue boiling for 10–12 minutes, or according to package directions. Pasta should be soft and completely cooked.
4. Drain the pasta and return to the pot, cooking over very low heat. Add the butter and parmesan, toss until completely melted.
5. Serve as finger food, or fork-mash if desired.

Spice It Up!

Feel free to enhance the flavors of a simple butter-pasta recipe with additional cheeses or spices. Try adding a dash of pepper and granulated garlic, for example, and stir in with the butter. Need a little color in this mostly yellow dish? Add a dash of paprika—it's fairly mild-flavored and adds a fun reddish tint.

Perfect Pasta with Carrot Peels

1 SERVING

¼ cup egg noodles
4 cups water
½ tablespoon butter or margarine
½ carrot

1. Bring the water to a rapid boil in a large saucepan.
2. While the water is boiling, wash and peel the carrot. Trim off both ends. Using a vegetable peeler, peel off strips of carrot and set aside.
3. Add pasta to the boiling water and stir to separate the noodles. Continue boiling for 10–12 minutes, or according to package directions. Pasta should be soft and completely cooked.
4. Drain the pasta and return to the pot, cooking over very low heat. Add the butter and carrots. Stir until the butter is melted, then toss to coat the pasta and carrots.
5. Serve as finger-food, or fork-mash if desired.

Rolled Pasta

A fun variation on this recipe is Rolled Pasta! Instead of egg noodles or spaghetti, boil 1–2 long lasagna noodles. When cooked, spread a bit of cream cheese on one side of a noodle. Then place carrot peels on the inside, and simply roll it up. Slice into 1-inch pieces, and serve as finger food.

Terrific Tomato Pasta

1 SERVING

½ cup uncooked pasta
4 cups water
½ tablespoon butter or
    margarine
¼ cup cherry tomatoes

⅛ teaspoon dill
1 tablespoon all-
    purpose flour
½ cup milk (regular
    or soy)

1. Bring the water to a boil in a medium saucepan. Add the pasta, then cook for 10–15 minutes.
2. Drain the pasta and return to the pot, cooking over very low heat. Add the butter and dill, tossing to coat the pasta.
3. In a small bowl, rapidly whisk the flour and milk together. When the flour is completely mixed in, slowly pour the mixture into the pasta.
4. Continue stirring the pasta until the sauce thickens.
5. Wash the cherry tomatoes and slice in half. Combine with the pasta and stir gently to mix.

Trade for Veggies

Save money on vegetables by setting up a vegetable exchange in your neighborhood. Most people with tomato or zucchini plants will usually be overrun with fresh produce during the high season. Plan to trade a bucket of apples from your tree, for example, for a box of fresh garden tomatoes.

Leafy and Lovely Greens
with Almonds

1 SERVING

1 cup fresh leafy greens
2 cups water
2 tablespoons sliced almonds
2 tablespoon butter or margarine

1. Wash the green leaves thoroughly, removing any damaged parts.
2. Steam in a small amount of water for about 10 minutes, or until the vegetables turn a bright green color.
3. Melt the butter in a small frying pan. Toast the almonds for about 5 minutes, stirring constantly to prevent burning.
4. When the almonds are toasted, mix with the spinach. Fork-mash if desired.

Spinach

This is a fun recipe that uses lots of spinach. Leafy green vegetables are some of the most beneficial ones out there. Most toddlers need little encouragement if they've been offered such vegetables from a young age. Almonds add a pleasant crunch, but don't substitute walnuts or peanuts; those nuts are larger and chunkier, and not safe for young children.

Scrumptious Baked Sweet Potatoes

2 SERVINGS

1 medium sweet potato or yam

1. Scrub the sweet potato thoroughly with a vegetable brush. Cut out any bad spots. Poke 8–10 holes into the potato, using a fork or other sharp implement.
2. Bake at 350°F for 1 hour, or until the potato skin is crispy.
3. When cooled, cut the potato in half. Scoop out the potato from the skin, and fork-mash if desired.

Too Dry

If your baked potatoes come out too dry, it's probably due to a combination of factors, starting with temperature. Cooking potatoes at 400°F makes the outside cook faster than the inside, leaving you with a burned skin and a hard, dry, undercooked middle. Also, look at the type of potato; yellow-fleshed potatoes tend to be dryer than their white-fleshed cousins.

A Lovely Couple,
Green Beans and Potatoes

1 SERVING

1 small new potato
½ cup green beans
2 cups chicken stock or water

1. Scrub the potato thoroughly with a vegetable brush. Cut out any bad spots, then dice into small pieces.
2. Wash the beans and snap off the ends. Cut into 1-inch segments.
3. Bring the chicken stock to boiling in a medium saucepan. Add the potatoes and cook for 15 minutes.
4. Add in the green beans and cook for another 8–10 minutes. If bright-green beans are too firm for baby, cook another 4–5 minutes; they will lose some of their color, but will be easier for toddlers to mash with their gums.
5. Drain the vegetables and serve as finger food. Fork-mash if desired.

Red, White, and Green

Potatoes and beans are a nice colorful dish. Toddlers will be drawn to the bright greens and whites, which may be a pleasant change from the monotone purées she used to get! If you're inspired, add some cooked red bell peppers to this mix for an even brighter combination of vegetables.

Best-Dressed Potato Salad

2 SERVINGS

2 red potatoes
4 cups water
1 tablespoon mayonnaise
1 tablespoon yogurt
½ teaspoon sugar
½ teaspoon prepared mustard
dash of salt
dash of garlic powder

1. Wash and peel the potatoes. Cut out any bad spots, then dice into small pieces.
2. Place the potatoes in a medium saucepan and cover with water. Bring to a boil and cook for 25–30 minutes, or until potatoes are soft.
3. Drain the potatoes and allow to cool.
4. In a small bowl, mix the mayonnaise, yogurt, sugar, mustard, garlic powder, and salt. Gently toss with the potatoes.
5. Chill before serving. Fork-mash if desired.

Hot or Cold?

Some potato salads are meant to be served hot, such as German potato salad. It's usually prepared with an oil-and-vinegar dressing, rather than the creamy dressing typical of cold potato salad. This variation may be a little too sour for your toddler, but it's certainly worth trying! Just be sure to serve it warm, not hot, to avoid burning your toddler's tongue.

Cheesy Twice-Baked Potatoes

2 SERVINGS

1 Russet potato
1 tablespoon cream cheese
1 ounce shredded Cheddar
½ tablespoon butter

1. Scrub the potato thoroughly with a vegetable brush. Cut out any bad spots.
2. Pat the potato dry with a paper towel, then poke 8–10 holes into the potato, using a fork or other sharp implement. Bake at 400°F for 1 hour.
3. Once the potato has cooled, slice it open and carefully remove the potato flesh.
4. Mix the potato with the Cheddar, cream cheese, and butter. Stir well, then put back inside the potato shell. Bake at 350°F for another 15–20 minutes.
5. Slice into strips before serving, or remove the potato skin entirely. Fork-mash if desired.

Potatoes

Twice-baked potatoes are a popular dish for the entire family, and a great way to use up leftover baked potatoes. When cooking for the rest of the family, you might incorporate bacon crumbles and diced green onion to the potato before rebaking, and also add a dash of salt and pepper.

Healthy Baked Fries, Oh My!

2 SERVINGS

1 medium red potato
1 teaspoon oil
⅛ teaspoon salt
⅛ teaspoon basil
½ teaspoon Parmesan ,optional

1. Preheat the oven to 400°F.
2. Wash and scrub the potato with a vegetable brush. Cut out any bad spots, then slice into strips.
3. Place the potatoes in a zippered plastic baggie. Add the oil, salt, basil, and cheese, and toss thoroughly to coat.
4. Spread the potatoes on a greased baking sheet. Bake for 15 minutes, then turn each fry over and bake for another 15 minutes. Fries should be cooked but not burned or overly crispy, as toddlers without a full set of teeth won't be able to chew them.
5. Allow fries to cool, then serve as finger food. Supervise closely to prevent choking.

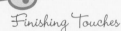

Finishing Touches

Many restaurants pour on the salt after their fries are finished cooking. The logic here is that the salt will adhere easily to a freshly oiled cooked potato. True, but toddlers don't need extra salt. Try seasoning the fries for toddlers before cooking; if the rest of the family complains that they're too bland, you can always add a dash of salt and paprika later.

Yummy Carrot-Yam Bake

2 SERVINGS

1 carrot
1 small yam or sweet potato
4 cups water
1 egg
1 tablespoon butter or margarine, melted
2 tablespoons milk (regular or soy)

1. Wash and peel the yam and carrot. Dice into chunks.
2. Place in a pot of water and bring to a boil. Cook for 30–35 minutes, or until soft.
3. Preheat oven to 350°F. Drain the vegetables and mash with a fork.
4. Beat the egg and milk together, then mix with the vegetables. Stir in the butter.
5. Bake in a greased ovenproof dish for 45 minutes, or until the vegetables are set and fully cooked. Allow to cool before serving.

Always Time for Pie

Fresh, warm pie has a special place in most people's hearts around the holidays, but there's no reason why toddlers can't enjoy this recipe year-round. It's essentially a sweet-potato pie minus the pie crust, which makes it a perfect dish for young eaters. If serving to grownups, add ½ cup of sugar and pour the mixture into a pie shell before baking.

Stupendous Spinach with Apples

1 SERVING

2 cups fresh leafy greens or ½ cup cooked
    spinach
½ apple
3 cups water

1. Wash the spinach leaves thoroughly, removing
   any damaged parts.
2. Wash and peel the apple, removing the core and
   seeds. Dice into small chunks.
3. Place the apple in a medium saucepan and cover
   with water. Bring to a boil and cook for 15–20
   minutes, or until apples are starting to soften.
4. Add the spinach and more water, if necessary.
   Return to a boil, then cook for 10–15 minutes,
   or until spinach is thoroughly cooked.
5. Fork-mash if desired.

The Salad Version

When making a grown-up dish using the same recipe,
how about a spinach and apple salad? Chop fresh spinach leaves and apples, and throw in ½ cup raisins and
walnuts. Serve with a light dressing of olive oil, bal-
samic vinegar, and a dash of salt, sugar, pepper, and
dry mustard.

Peachy Sweet Potatoes

2 SERVINGS

1 small peach
1 small yam or sweet potato, diced
4 cups water
⅛ teaspoon nutmeg
⅛ teaspoon cinnamon
⅛ teaspoon sugar

1. Place in a pot of water and bring to a boil. Cook for about 15 minutes.
2. Wash and peel the peach. Cut into thin slices and add to the pot with the sweet potato. Cook for another 15–20 minutes. Sprinkle the cinnamon, sugar, and nutmeg into the cooking water.
3. When cooked, drain the peach and sweet potato and allow to cool. Serve as finger food or fork-mash if desired.

Cinnamon

While straight cinnamon smells fantastic, it usually has a slightly bitter taste. To get the flavor of the cinnamon without the bitter overtone, recipes almost always instruct mixing it with sugar. By the same token, although nutmeg smells fantastic, a little goes a long way, and without a touch of something sweet, too much nutmeg will make for a bitter meal.

Perfectly Smashed Potatoes

1 SERVING

1 red potato, diced
1 tablespoon oil
3 cups water
dash of salt and pepper, optional

1. Place diced potato in a saucepan, cover with water, and bring to a boil. Cook for 30–35 minutes, or until soft.
2. Drain the potatoes. Heat the oil in the saucepan and add the potatoes again. When they start to brown, smash with a fork or potato masher. If desired, add a dash of salt and pepper while smashing.
3. Allow to cool before serving.

Fun Potatoes

Smashed potatoes are typically lumpier than mashed potatoes and are often browned in a pan before serving. A two-year-old may have fun with the one-sided crispiness of the smashed potatoes.

Adventurous Peas with Mint

1 SERVING

½ cup peas
2 cups water
3 leaves fresh mint
½ tablespoon butter

1. Chop the fresh mint into tiny pieces.
2. Place the peas in a pot of water and bring to a boil. Cook for 8–10 minutes, or until the peas are soft.
3. Drain the water and return the peas to the pot. Add the butter, stirring constantly until the butter melts.
4. Add the chopped mint and mix. Serve as-is or fork-mash if desired.

Mint

Mint is both refreshing and medicinal. If your toddler has an upset stomach or seems irritable from gas, adding a bit of mint to his diet may be just the thing. Mint may have a curative effect on nausea, headache, and other various ailments. Plus, it smells great while cooking and tastes even better.

Delightful Asparagus Cheese Dip

1 SERVING

2 asparagus spears
2 cups of water
½ ripe avocado
1 tablespoon cottage cheese

1. Bring the asparagus and water to a boil in a shallow saucepan. Steam for 10–15 minutes, or until asparagus is soft.
2. Cut the avocado in half. Remove the pit and scoop the avocado out of the skin. Cut into chunks and place in a food processor or blender.
3. When the asparagus is cooked, chop into pieces and add to the food processor.
4. Add the cottage cheese to the food processor and purée until the mixture is smooth. If it's too thick, add cooking water from the asparagus, one tablespoon at a time.
5. Serve as a dipping sauce. Refrigerate the leftovers immediately.

Dippers

Toddlers may want to dip their fingers (or entire hands) into this recipe—and that's okay! But if you're looking for a cleaner dipper than a human body part, try the homemade wheat crackers on page 83. Bread crusts make excellent tools for dipping. Also, try well-cooked baby carrots as dippers; they're firm enough for toddlers to handle, and soft enough to chew.

Red Tomato Risotto

1 SERVING

½ cup Arborio rice
1 tablespoon butter or margarine
½ cup tomato
⅔ cup chicken stock or water
¼ cup grated Parmesan, optional

1. Wash the tomato and dice into small pieces. Alternatively, use canned diced tomatoes, and manually dice into smaller pieces. Reserve all juices.
2. Bring the chicken stock and tomatoes to a boil. Add the rice and reduce heat to simmering.
3. Cover and cook for 20–25 minutes, or until all liquid is absorbed. When preparing this dish for older children or adults, cook the risotto about 5 minutes less so the rice is firmer.
4. Stir in the Parmesan once the rice is fully cooked. Either serve as-is or fork-mash if desired.

Risotto

The best thing about risotto is that it's soft—perfect for toddlers without a full mouthful of teeth. The sauce is cooked right into the rice, yielding an easy-to-make dish that's very flavorful. While usually made with Arborio rice, risotto can also be made with carnaroli or vialone nano. These are particularly starchy grains that give risotto its creamy texture.

Cheese Colcannon Concoction

1 SERVING

1 medium red potato
3 cups water
½ cup fresh spinach leaves
1 cabbage leaf
1 ounce Cheddar, shredded

1. Wash and peel the potato. Dice.
2. Place the potato in a medium saucepan and cover with water. Bring to a boil, then cook for about 20 minutes.
3. Add the cabbage and spinach into the saucepan. Return to a boil, then continue cooking for another 10 minutes.
4. Drain the vegetables, then fork-mash until they are combined.
5. Add in the shredded cheese and continue fork-mashing until the cheese is incorporated.

Hold the Mace

Traditional colcannon is seasoned with mace, an Indonesian spice that is similar to nutmeg (and actually comes from the same tree as nutmeg). Mace may be difficult to find, can be expensive, and its flavor isn't always one that young children find appealing. If you're inclined, try adding ⅛ teaspoon while fork-mashing the vegetables together.

Chickadee Chickpea and Tomato Salad

2 SERVINGS

½ cup canned garbanzo beans
½ cup tomato
1 tablespoon parsley
1 teaspoon olive oil
1 teaspoon red wine vinegar
½ teaspoon sugar
¼ teaspoon lemon juice

1. Drain the garbanzo beans and rinse well.
2. Wash the tomato and remove the stem and any tough white flesh. Dice into small pieces.
3. In a small bowl, mix together the oil, vinegar, sugar, and lemon juice.
4. Toss the dressing with the garbanzo beans and tomatoes. Fork-mash before serving. If your toddler seems averse to the sourness of the vinegar, either omit it or skip the dressing entirely.

Garbanzo Beans

Garbanzo beans, also called chickpeas, are a great staple for toddlers because they're mild in flavor and high in protein. This is also an easy summer dish because it can be served raw—no cooking required! Cooking the tomatoes will soften them, so feel free to cook them for 10–15 minutes before using. Be sure to fork-mash thoroughly.

Clever Carrot Pancakes

4 SERVINGS

1 carrot
1 cup all-purpose flour
½ cup milk or water
1 egg
4 teaspoons oil
1 teaspoon baking powder

1. Wash and peel the carrot, and remove both ends.
   Grate the remainder.
2. Mix the flour, egg, baking powder, and 1 teaspoon oil in a medium bowl. When it forms a
   batter, stir in the grated carrot.
3. Heat 1 tablespoon of oil in a frying pan. Drop
   spoonfuls of batter into the heated oil. The
   resulting pancakes should be 1–2 inches in
   diameter. Cook 2–3 minutes, or until browned.
   Flip and cook 2–3 minutes on the other side.
4. Drain onto paper towels. Serve as finger food
   once cooled.

Up the Protein

Looking for a good way to increase the protein in your
child's diet? Try adding cooked chickpeas to the grated
carrots before frying. Simply purée ½ cup chickpeas
in the food processor, then mix by hand with the carrots and form small patties. They taste delicious and
provide a healthy meat alternative.

Baby's Veggie Casserole

3 SERVINGS

½ cup broccoli
½ cup zucchini
½ cup cauliflower
1 small carrot

4 cups water
1 tablespoon butter
½ cup shredded
Cheddar

1. Wash the broccoli and cauliflower. Dice into small florets.
2. Wash and peel carrot, and dice into small coins.
3. Put carrot in a medium saucepan. Add 3 cups of water, bring to a boil, and cook for 10 minutes. Add the broccoli, cauliflower, and zucchini and cook another 10–15 minutes, or until the vegetables are soft.
4. Drain the vegetables, then add the butter and cheese. Stir until melted, tossing the vegetables to ensure an even coating.
5. Pour into a greased dish about the size of a loaf pan. Bake at 350°F for 30 minutes. Allow to cool, then either serve as-is or fork-mash if desired.

Casserole

Vegetable casseroles can be prepared in any number of ways. Many have crunchy toppings, which are great for older kids but less appropriate for toddlers. If you like, crush up some butter-flavored crackers and place on top of half the dish. Dot with butter, then bake for the same amount of time. Half the dish will be fine for a toddler, and half will be suited for an older audience.

Nifty Broccoli and Cheese Nuggets

3 SERVINGS

¾ cup broccoli
2 cups water
½ cup Mozzarella
1 egg

¼ cup bread crumbs
2 tablespoons oil

1. Wash the broccoli and dice. Cover with water in a saucepan and bring to a boil. Cook for 15 minutes. Drain and let cool, then either purée in a food processor or fork-mash.
2. Grate Mozzarella, and mix it with the broccoli. Pour in a beaten egg and combine.
3. Tightly mold a small ball of broccoli and cheese. Roll it in bread crumbs and place on a plate. Repeat until all the balls are made.
4. Fry balls in oil for 1–2 minutes on each side. Cool and drain.

It's All in the Oil

There are several types of oil you can use for cooking. Canola oil is relatively high in monounsaturated fat and low in saturated fat, so it is an excellent choice for cooking. Vegetable oil (which is generally made from soybean oil) is less high in the "good fat." Sunflower oil has a high amount of protein, and is particularly good for frying.

Terrific Tuna with Vegetables

2 SERVINGS

2 ounces canned tuna	1 tablespoon butter
½ cup peas	dash garlic powder
½ cup carrots	2 cups water

1. Drain tuna and mash into small pieces.
2. Wash and peel the carrot, then dice into small pieces. Place in a saucepan, cover with water, and bring to a boil. Cook for about 10 minutes.
3. Add the peas to the pot and cook for another 10–12 minutes, or until vegetables are tender. Toss with a dash of garlic powder.
4. Grease a small ovenproof baking dish. Combine tuna and cooked vegetables and spread in dish. Dot with butter. Bake at 350°F for about 20 minutes, or until the fish is heated through.
5. Allow to cool, then either serve as-is or fork-mash if desired.

Fish and Mercury Warning

White albacore tuna comes from larger fish and can be higher in mercury than chunk light tuna. It is safe to feed your baby tuna once or twice a week, and it's better to stick to chunk light tuna than albacore. Avoid shark, swordfish, king mackerel, and tilefish—these large fish commonly have high levels of mercury.

Fresh Baked Fish Sticks

I SERVING

1 white fish fillet	¼ cup all-purpose
1 egg	flour
½ cup milk	1 tablespoon
¼ cup bread crumbs	Parmesan cheese

1. Preheat oven to 400°F. Grease a baking sheet or dish.
2. Rinse the fish fillet and remove all bones. Cut into slices.
3. Beat the egg and milk together in a small bowl. Place the flour in a pile on one small plate, and the bread crumbs in a pile on another small plate.
4. Dip each fish stick into flour, then egg, then bread crumbs. Shake gently to remove any excess and place on the baking sheet.
5. Bake for 15–18 minutes. Flip the fish sticks over halfway during cooking. Cool before serving as finger-food.

Checking Out the Locals

If you eat locally caught fish, make sure to check any warnings about mercury that might be available for fish in your area. If no warnings are available, stick to 1–2 meals of local fish per week.

Ground Turkey, a Healthy Choice

2 SERVINGS

4 ounces turkey, ground
1 tablespoon onion, diced
⅛ teaspoon prepared mustard
½ tablespoon oil

1. Heat the oil in a frying pan. Add onion and sauté for 4–5 minutes, or until the onion is translucent.
2. Mix the turkey and mustard in a small bowl. Add to the frying pan and sauté for 8–10 minutes, or until the meat is completely cooked.
3. Allow to cool, then either serve as-is or fork-mash if desired.

Turkey Combinations

Because of its low fat content, ground turkey can be drier than fattier meats like ground beef. For this reason, especially with small children, it's a good idea to add it into a sauce. If preparing "standalone" ground turkey into patties, add liquid ingredients such as Worcestershire sauce, prepared mustard, or milk—they will make the meat more tender.

Something New: Chicken with Bananas

2 SERVINGS

1 small boneless, skinless chicken breast
     (about 6 ounces)
1 banana
2 tablespoons butter, melted

1. Preheat the oven to 350°F. Wash the chicken breast and remove any skin or fat.
2. Brush both sides of the breast with butter. Place in a greased dish.
3. Peel the banana and remove any damaged spots. Cut into thin slices and place on top of the chicken. Drizzle the remaining melted butter on top of the bananas.
4. Bake for 30 minutes, or until the chicken's internal temperature reaches 170 degrees and the juice from the chicken runs clear when pricked with a fork.
5. Allow to cool, then cut into small pieces and serve. You can also fork-mash if desired.

Bananas

We often think of bananas as breakfast and snack foods, but why not for lunch or dinner too? Many Caribbean cultures cook with bananas on a regular basis. Try this simple chicken and banana recipe, which is sure to appeal to a banana-loving toddler.

Happy Ham and Peaches

1 SERVING

3 ounces ham, cooked
½ ripe peach
1 tablespoon butter
1 teaspoon honey

1. Wash the peach and cut in half. Peel the half you're using for this recipe, remove the pit, and dice into small pieces. Either cut a wedge out of a ham steak, use leftovers from a baked ham, or use 2 thin slices of deli-style ham.
2. Melt the butter in a medium skillet. Add the ham and sauté for several minutes, or until both sides are lightly browned. Add the honey and continue cooking another 1–2 minutes.
3. Add the diced peach to the skillet. Cook for 4–5 minutes, stirring constantly to prevent sticking or burning. Allow to cool, then either serve as-is or fork-mash if desired.

Honey

Make sure that honey is only served to children older than 12 months old because there's a risk of botulism for younger babies. Honey is okay for toddlers and older children.

Cordon Bleu for You!

2 SERVINGS

1 small boneless, skinless chicken breast (6 oz)
2 thin slices of ham
2 ounces cheese, shredded

2 tablespoons bread crumbs
1 tablespoon butter, melted

1. Preheat the oven to 350°F. Wash the chicken breast and remove any skin or fat.
2. Slice the chicken breast in half horizontally. Pound thin with a meat mallet.
3. Place the ham slices over one piece of chicken. Sprinkle the cheese on top, then place the other piece of chicken on top.
4. Place the assembly in a greased baking dish. Brush with melted butter then sprinkle the top with bread crumbs. Bake for 40 minutes, or until the chicken's internal temperature reaches 170 degrees. The juice from the chicken should run clear when pricked with a fork. Cool, cut into pieces and serve. You can also fork-mash if desired.

Stuffed Chicken

When making a stuffed chicken or stuffed beef dish, a meat mallet is important because it will both flatten and tenderize the meat. A meat mallet is basically a perforated wooden or metal block, usually attached to a wooden handle. Simply place the meat on an appropriate work surface, then pound it with the mallet.

Chicken with Spinach

2 SERVINGS

1 small boneless, skinless chicken breast
 (about 6 ounces)
1 tablespoon oil
1 cup fresh spinach (or ¼ cup pre-cooked)
¼ teaspoon parsley
½ cup chicken stock or water
⅛ teaspoon pepper

1. Wash the chicken breast and remove any fat.
   Dice into small pieces.
2. Heat the oil in a non-stick skillet or wok. Add
   the chicken and stir-fry for 8–10 minutes or until
   chicken is no longer pink in the middle.
3. Add the spinach, chicken stock, parsley, and
   pepper. Continue to stir-fry an additional 4–5
   minutes.
4. Allow to cool, then either serve as-is or fork-mash
   if desired.

Add the Flavor In!

A quick way to add a little flavor to stir-fried chicken is
to add a little sesame oil with the cooking oil. This will
give the meal a great roasted-sesame flavor, without
having to add sesame seeds (which are small enough
not to be a choking hazard, but require careful attention for roasting).

Fantastic Yogurt Fruit Drink

2 SERVINGS

1 cup vanilla yogurt
2 strawberries
1 peach
½ banana

1. Hull and clean the strawberries. Cut in half.
2. Wash and peel the peach. Remove the pit, cut into pieces.
3. Peel the banana and remove any damaged spots. Cut into chunks.
4. Place strawberries, peach, banana, and yogurt in the blender. Mix until a thin drink results.
5. Add water as needed, 1 tablespoon at a time, if too thick.

Healthy Substitutions

Here is a healthy summer drink. It could even be made into a winter drink! Simply substitute whatever fruit is in season—it's hard to go wrong with puréed fruit and yogurt. If you're out of fruit, use fruit juice instead.

Fun Fruit Slush

1 SERVING

¼ cup frozen orange juice concentrate
¼ cup frozen lemonade concentrate
½ banana
¼ cup raspberries or strawberries
½ cup water

1. Mix the fruit juice concentrates and water into a freezer-safe bowl or cup.
2. Peel the banana and remove any damaged spots. Fork-mash and mix into the cup of juice and water.
3. Freeze for at least 1 hour.
4. When ready to serve, thaw to the "slush stage" and stir.

Alternates

A more traditional method of making fruit slushes is to put ice cubes and various fruits into a blender. Frozen juice concentrate, on the other hand, is faster to prepare but generally requires more waiting time while the concentrates either freeze or thaw to the right consistency.

Best Banana Smoothie

1 SERVING

½ ripe banana
½ cup vanilla yogurt (regular or soy)
½ cup orange juice

1. Peel the banana and remove any damaged spots. Cut into slices and place in a blender or food processor.
2. Add the juice and yogurt.
3. Blend until the drink is completely smooth.
4. Refrigerate any leftover drink immediately.

For the Older Crowd

If you're whipping up this drink for grownups, there are a couple of small additions you could make to improve on the flavor and texture. Try using crushed ice instead of orange juice, and add a touch of banana liqueur. You can also add a bit of lemon juice, or serve it with a slice of lemon in the glass—the acidity will make a pleasing contrast to the banana.

Very Berry Smoothie

2 SERVINGS

½ *ripe banana*
½ *cup yogurt (regular or soy)*
¼ *cup apple juice*
2 *large strawberries*
¼ *cup raspberries or blueberries*

1. Peel the banana and remove any damaged spots. Cut into slices and place in a blender or food processor.
2. Wash the berries and remove all stems. Cut in half and place in the food processor. You can use either frozen or fresh berries.
3. Add the juice and yogurt.
4. Blend until the drink is completely smooth.
5. Refrigerate any leftover drink immediately

Why Banana?

Bananas are in most smoothie recipes because they help with the texture—they make a smoothie thicker and creamier than it would be with only yogurt. Without banana, a smoothie would be more of a slushie, or an iced fruit drink.

Mouthwatering Melon Smoothie

2 SERVINGS

⅓ cup honeydew   *⅓ cup watermelon*
⅓ cup cantaloupe   *½ cup apple juice*

1. Cut the honeydew in half and remove all seeds. Cut out about ⅓ cup of melon chunks. Place in a food processor or blender.
2. Cut the cantaloupe in half and remove all seeds. Cut out about ⅓ cup of melon chunks. Add to the food processor.
3. Take a wedge of watermelon and remove all seeds, both white and black. Cut out ⅓ cup of chunks and add to the food processor.
4. Add the apple juice and blend until the drink is completely smooth. If the drink is too thick, add more juice by the tablespoon. If it's too thin, add more fruit or a tablespoon of yogurt.
5. Refrigerate any leftover drink immediately.

Melon

If melon isn't in season, don't despair. Frozen melon is just fine for making a frozen fruit drink. You can also make your own frozen fruit! Next time you buy a watermelon, cut up a few cups worth into chunks and pop it into the freezer. That way, you'll have fruit ready to use whenever you need it.

Simply Delicious
Chocolate Chip Cookies

6 SERVINGS

1 egg	¾ cup all-purpose flour
½ cup shortening	¼ teaspoon salt
⅓ cup white sugar	½ teaspoon baking soda
⅓ cup brown sugar, packed	1 cup chocolate chips
	1 cup ground oats

1. Preheat the oven to 350°F.
2. In a medium bowl, cream the shortening and sugar together. Mix with a fork until large crumbles are formed, or use an electric mixer.
3. Add the egg and mix well. Add in the flour, salt, and baking soda, continuing to stir until a dough is formed. Add oatmeal and chocolate chips. Stir well, then drop spoonfuls onto a greased baking sheet, leaving about 2 inches between each cookie. Bake for 11–14 minutes.
4. Let cool on the baking sheet for 1–2 minutes, then remove and finish cooling on wire racks.

Chewy Versus Hard

When making cookies for toddlers, try to bake them on the soft side (rather than hard and crunchy). Don't overdo it on the baking powder or baking soda, since those ingredients tend to make cookies more cake-like. Don't overcook; burning is a sure way to crisp a cookie. For really soft cookies, try using corn syrup instead of sugar.

Tasty Oatmeal Cookies

5 SERVINGS

1 egg
½ cup shortening
¼ cup white sugar
½ cup brown sugar,
    packed
½ teaspoon vanilla
    extract

½ cup all-purpose flour
¼ teaspoon salt
½ teaspoon baking soda
1½ cups rolled
    oats (quick or
    old-fashioned)
⅛ teaspoon cinnamon

1. Preheat the oven to 350°F.
2. In a medium bowl, cream the shortening and sugars together. Mix with a fork until large crumbles are formed, or use an electric mixer.
3. Add the egg and vanilla, mixing well. Add in the flour, cinnamon, salt, and baking soda, continuing to stir until a dough is formed.
4. Add oatmeal. Stir well, then drop spoonfuls onto a greased baking sheet, leaving about 2 inches between each cookie. Bake for 9–11 minutes.
5. Let cool on the baking sheet for 1–2 minutes, then remove and cool on wire racks.

Oatmeal Varieties

Chewy and delicious, oatmeal cookies can have varieties that are limited only by your imagination. Once your toddler grows older, you can add dried fruit, nuts, and other tasty surprises.

Chapter 6

Growing, Growing, Gone!

INVOLVING LITTLE ONES IN food preparation creates the kind of pride of accomplishment that can bring about a willingness to eat their creations. Include toddlers in decision-making too. For instance, "Do you want to put green or black olives on the salads?" and let them dip their (washed) fingers into the jar to add some to the plates. At mealtime, be sure you gush your compliments to the chef! It only takes a few minutes spent together in the kitchen each day— by the time youngsters are three, they will be able to make a substantial contribution. In the long run, parents will be paid back with interest for the time and extra work kiddie "help" costs them now.

24–36 Months

As your child starts to identify which foods are his/her favorite, it's tempting to stick to staple meals. But keep experimenting with your little one. The meals in this chapter resemble what you may put on your adult dinner table, but with special twists. Keep trying new things and your child is bound to find some new favorites!

For the Love of Meatloaf

4 SERVINGS

½ pound ground beef
¼ cup milk or water
1 egg
2 tablespoons ketchup
1 teaspoon Worcester-
    shire sauce

¼ teaspoon oregano
¼ teaspoon parsley
dash of salt and
    pepper
¼ cup bread crumbs
½ small onion, diced

1. Preheat the oven to 350°F.
2. In a medium bowl, mix the ground beef, egg, and milk together. Stir well.
3. Add in the ketchup, Worcestershire, oregano, parsley, salt, pepper, bread crumbs, and onions. Mix thoroughly to combine, using your hands if necessary.
4. Place in an oven-proof baking dish and cook at 350°F for 1 hour. Allow to cool before slicing and serving.

To Sauce or Not to Sauce

A fun alternative to standard meatloaf is to coat it with a glaze. Pour ½ cup tomato sauce over the top, spread with a spoon, and bake. If tomato sauce is scarce, ketchup or honey-mustard sauce is a good substitute.

Creamy Chicken and Potatoes

4 SERVINGS

1 small potato, cubed
1 cup water
4 teaspoons butter or
    margarine
2 teaspoons all-purpose
    flour

½ cup milk
½ cup cooked chicken,
    cubed
2 tablespoons grated
    cheese

1. Peel potato and cut into cubes. Place potato in pot with water. Bring to boil, reduce heat, and simmer until tender, about 10–15 minutes. Remove from pot and drain.
2. In a small pan, melt butter over low heat. When melted, stir in flour until well mixed. Add milk and whisk until smooth.
3. Cook over low heat. Stir often to thicken.
4. Add potato and chicken, and stir. Remove pot from heat, add cheese, and let cool.

Practice Makes Perfect

This simple, creamy dish combines cubes of chicken and potatoes with a creamy, cheesy sauce. Just the thing for your child to practice using his new fork on!

Turkey with a Fruity Twist

1 SERVING

½ cup cooked turkey
2 large lettuce leaves
¼ cup grapes
¼ cup cantaloupe or
    honeydew melon
1 ounce Mozzarella or
    Cheddar, shredded

1 teaspoon olive oil
1 teaspoon white wine
    vinegar
dash prepared mustard

1. Tear the lettuce into small pieces and place in the bottom of a serving bowl.
2. Cut the turkey into small pieces, removing any fat and skin. Place on top of the lettuce.
3. Wash the grapes and cut in half. Cut the melon into small cubes. Mix grapes and melon in with the turkey. Top with shredded cheese.
4. Prepare the dressing by mixing the oil, vinegar, and mustard. Stir well, then drizzle over the salad and mix gently.

Grown-Up Salad Dressing

Many children will eat vegetables with the "modified" oil-and-vinegar dressing described here. To make this dressing more suitable for adult taste buds, add a dash of garlic powder, salt, pepper, sugar, and freshly diced herbs.

Everyone Should Eat Meatballs

5 SERVINGS

1 egg
¼ cup milk or water
1 teaspoon Worcester-
    shire sauce
1 pound ground beef

¾ cup bread crumbs
1 teaspoon paprika
dash of salt and
    pepper
½ small onion, diced

1. Preheat the oven to 375°F.
2. In a medium bowl, mix the egg, Worcestershire, and milk together. Beat thoroughly.
3. Add in the ground beef, bread crumbs, paprika, salt, pepper, and onions.
4. Form mixture into balls about 1 inch in diameter.
5. Place the meatballs onto a baking sheet with sides or in a deep baking dish. Bake at 375°F for 30–40 minutes, or until the meat is no longer pink.

Meatballs
A true family favorite, meatballs go well with boxed pasta or Homemade Egg Pasta (page 122). They can also be served with steamed vegetables for a lower-carbohydrate meal.

Scrumptious Stuffed Peppers

2 SERVINGS

1 large bell pepper
¼ pound ground beef
¼ cup tomato sauce
¼ cup cooked white or brown rice
1 ounce cheese, shredded
dash of salt and pepper

1. Preheat the oven to 350°F
2. Wash the pepper and cut off the top. Remove all seeds from the cavity.
3. Brown the ground beef in a skillet over medium heat for 10 minutes, or until it's completely cooked. Drain any fat and return beef to the pan.
4. Mix the rice, tomato sauce, cheese, salt, and pepper in with the beef. Continue cooking over low heat for 3–4 minutes, or until the cheese is melted.
5. Place the bell pepper in a deep baking dish. Pour the meat mixture inside, then bake for 1 hour, or until the green pepper is tender.

Rice Instead

Bell peppers can be stuffed with a variety of fillings. If your toddler doesn't like meat, try stuffing the peppers with rice, cheese, and tomatoes instead. Or, for a southwestern twist, make a filling with corn, onions, tomatoes, and a dash of chili powder.

Fancy-Filled Pork Chop

2 SERVINGS

1 pork chop
¼ cup applesauce
1 tablespoon soy sauce
1 small clove garlic, peeled

1. Preheat the oven to 350°F.
2. Wash the pork chop and remove the bone. Using a sharp knife, slice the chop in half horizontally about ¾ of the way through the chop.
3. Stuff the applesauce into the cavity.
4. Place the pork in an ovenproof baking dish. Spoon the soy sauce and garlic over the top, and bake for 40–50 minutes, or until the pork's internal temperature reaches 165 degrees.
5. Remove the garlic and discard. Slice pork into small pieces before serving.

Pork Roast

An easy way to expand this recipe for a larger group of eaters is to make it with a pork roast instead of a pork chop. Simply increase the amount of applesauce in proportion to the larger size of the pork roast.

Terrific Tomato and Hamburger Sauce

2 SERVINGS

¼ pound ground beef
¼ cup stewed tomatoes, diced
⅛ cup tomato sauce
⅛ cup chopped green pepper
dash of chili powder
dash of salt and pepper

1. Brown the ground beef in a skillet over medium heat for 10–15 minutes, or until completely cooked.
2. Drain any fat and return the meat to the pan.
3. Add in the tomato, green pepper, tomato sauce, chili powder, salt, and pepper. Stir well, then simmer for 10–15 minutes.

Round It Out

To turn the Tomato and Hamburger recipe into a full meal, simply add pasta! Cook about ½ cup of pasta in boiling water for 15–20 minutes or until cooked, then serve with the hamburger sauce. If you're a vegetarian, try making this recipe with kidney beans or black beans instead of hamburger. Skip the browning stage and go right to the simmering.

Turkey Dinner for Any Night

1 SERVING

1 ounce ground turkey	1 tablespoon butter
½ cup green beans	1 cup water
1 small carrot, diced	
¼ cup rice	

1. Wash the green beans and snap off the ends. Cut into 1-inch-long segments.
2. Brown the turkey in a skillet over medium heat for 10–15 minutes, or until it's completely cooked.
3. Drain any fat and return the turkey to the skillet.
4. Add the water and butter. Bring to a boil, then add in the rice, beans, and carrots. Reduce to a simmer and cook for 30 minutes, or until rice is cooked and fluffy.
5. Check periodically to ensure that there's enough liquid. If the rice starts sticking before it's done, add ¼ cup water. Let cool before serving, and fork-mash if desired.

Thanksgiving All Year

Make your toddler a simple Thanksgiving dinner any time of year! This is a convenient one-skillet meal that can easily be made with leftovers.

Autumn Lamb with Apple

2 SERVINGS

1–2 ounces of boneless lamb
1 apple, diced
1 tablespoon butter
1 teaspoon turmeric
¼ teaspoon paprika
⅛ teaspoon cinnamon

1. Cut the lamb into small pieces. Melt the butter in a skillet, then add the lamb and sauté until the meat is completely cooked, about 8–10 minutes.
2. Add the apple, turmeric, paprika, and cinnamon. Continue stir-frying for 2–3 minutes.
3. Preheat the oven to 350°F. Grease an oven-proof baking dish, then pour the lamb-and-apple mixture into a greased baking dish. Bake for 30 minutes.
4. Allow to cool before serving.

Selection Tips

When selecting a good cut of beef for serving to toddlers, marbled cuts are a good choice because they are generally more tender. Not so with lamb! Because the animal is less mature, lamb is usually quite tender and doesn't require the marbled fat that beef does to make the meat tender.

Sweet-and-Sour Meatballs

2 SERVINGS

¼ pound ground beef
2 teaspoons oil
½ cup canned pineapple chunks, diced
¼ cup bell pepper, diced

½ teaspoon soy sauce
¼ cup bread crumbs
1 teaspoon cornstarch
2 tablespoons water

1. Mix the ground beef, bread crumbs, and soy sauce together. Form into round 1-inch balls.
2. Heat the oil in a skillet. Add the meatballs, reduce heat to medium, and cook until the meatballs are no longer pink.
3. Put the pineapple chunks and juice (about ¼ cup) into a small bowl. Add cornstarch and water, then stir well to mix. Add in the bell pepper.
4. Pour the pineapple mixture into the skillet. Stir the meatballs around to coat in the sauce, and cook the sauce for several minutes or until it thickens.
5. Allow to cool before serving.

Keeping It Together

If your meatballs always fall apart when you cook on the stovetop, there are a few things you can try to help them maintain their shape. Add a little oil to the pan to keep them from sticking and falling apart when you roll them over. Also, adding more egg and bread crumbs (and pressing the meat very firmly into balls) will keep them from disintegrating into meat sauce.

Chicken, Pasta, and Carrots Trio

2 SERVINGS

*1 small boneless, skin-
    less chicken breast
    (about 6 ounces)*
½ cup pasta

1 medium carrot
2 teaspoons oil
½ cup chicken stock

1. Wash the chicken breast and remove any skin or fat. Cut into small pieces.
2. Heat the oil in a skillet. Add the chicken, then stir-fry for 10–12 minutes, or until the chicken is cooked.
3. Wash and peel the carrot; slice into thin coins.
4. Bring water to a boil. Add the carrots and cook for about 10 minutes. Add the pasta and cook for another 20 minutes, or until both pasta and carrots are tender.
5. Drain, then add the pasta and carrots into the skillet with the chicken. Add chicken stock and cook at a high temperature for 4–5 minutes.

Spoon, Fork, or Spork?

Your toddler has 3 main choices for feeding implements once her fingers no longer suffice. Rubber-tipped spoons are great for feeding purées, and dull-tined forks help more for stabbing discreet bites. Neither seeming to work quite well enough? Try a spork, or a spoon with tined edges. She can both scoop and stab at the same time.

Shepherd's Pie

4 SERVINGS

½ pound ground beef   1 tablespoon butter
½ cup peas   ½ cup milk or water
2 medium russet   6 cups water
   potatoes

1. Wash, peel, and cut the potatoes into chunks. Bring 4 cups of water to a boil. Add the potatoes and cook for 25–30 minutes or until soft.
2. Brown beef in a skillet until completely cooked, about 10–15 minutes. Drain. Bring 1 cup of water to a boil in a small saucepan. Add the peas and cook for 8–10 minutes.
3. Place the drained potatoes in a bowl. Add the butter and begin mashing. Add milk, 1 tablespoon at a time, until creamy.
4. Place the ground beef and peas in a greased baking dish. Spread the mashed potatoes on top, then bake at 350°F for about 1 hour.

Leftovers

Shepherd's Pie is a traditional meal consisting of beef and vegetables, topped with mashed potatoes, and baked. Any leftover meat will work.

Ham and Potato Patties

3 SERVINGS

1 cup cooked ham, chopped
2 medium red potatoes
4 cups water
1 egg
dash of pepper
1 tablespoon oil

1. Peel potatoes, then grate into a medium bowl. Mix grated potato with the ham and pepper.
2. Beat the egg, then pour into the ham-and-potato mixture and stir thoroughly to combine. Form into patties.
3. Heat the oil, and cook the patties for 3–4 minutes per side, or until lightly browned. Drain on paper towels before serving.

Ham Hash Browns

Another way to make ham and potato patties is to make Ham Hash Browns. Grate slice the cooked ham into very thin strips, then mix with grated potato and fry it in one large patty. You can even prepare the mixture the night before, store it in the refrigerator, then cook up for a hearty morning's breakfast.

Baked Chicken Nuggets They'll Love

2 SERVINGS

1 small boneless, skin-
    less chicken breast
    (about 6 ounces)
1 cup bread crumbs or
    corn flakes

½ teaspoon garlic
    powder
¼ teaspoon onion
    powder
¼ teaspoon parsley

1. Wash the chicken breast and remove any skin or fat. Cut into bite-sized pieces.
2. If using corn flakes, crush into a fine powder. Add the parsley, garlic powder, and onion powder to bread crumbs or crushed corn flakes, and mix well.
3. Roll each piece of chicken in the crushed flakes or bread crumbs. Set on a plate.
4. Preheat the oven to 400°F. Place the breaded nuggets on a greased baking sheet and cook for about 15 minutes, or until the chicken is white when you slice into it.

Keep It Healthy

Here's a healthy solution to fried chicken nuggets. They take a little longer to bake than to pan- or deep-fry, but they're less greasy and healthier for the whole family.

Mini Pizza Faces

2 SERVINGS

1 English muffin	4 thin slices pepperoni
2 tablespoons tomato sauce	1 baby carrot
1 ounce shredded Mozzarella	2 tablespoons peas
	2 cups water

1. Preheat oven to 375°F.
2. Slice the baby carrot in half lengthwise. Place it and the peas in a saucepan with the water. Bring to a boil, then cook for about 10 minutes, or until the vegetables are tender. Drain and set aside.
3. Split the English muffin in half and lay the two pieces face-up on a baking sheet. Spoon tomato sauce over each muffin to cover it.
4. On each muffin, place 2 pieces of pepperoni for eyes. Place half a baby carrot for a nose. Make a smile out of peas. Place the shredded Mozzarella around the top of the muffin for hair.
5. Bake for 10–15 minutes, or until the cheese melts.

Super-Size It
If the whole family's in the mood for pizza, simply make a full-sized pie and serve your toddler a slice. Use the same fun ingredients to make a pizza face, but use pizza dough instead of English muffins.

Creamed Tuna on Toasty Bread

1 SERVING

¼ cup chunk light tuna
½ cup milk (regular or soy)
1 tablespoon all-purpose flour
1 tablespoon butter
1 piece whole-grain bread

1. Melt the butter in a small saucepan.
2. Add the flour, stirring constantly until dissolved. Add the milk and continue stirring until it forms a thick sauce.
3. Turn off the heat and add the tuna. Stir until mixed and creamy.
4. Serve on top of a piece of whole-grain toast.

A Sweet Touch

Creamed fish recipes can be made a little sweeter by adding a touch of sugar to the white sauce. On the other hand, some prefer a dash of salt with their tuna. You can also make this meal more visually appealing by adding a handful of peas for color. Again, be careful about serving tuna too often because of the amount of mercury in it.

Fish Lover's Chowder

2 SERVINGS

1 boneless fillet white fish

1 tablespoon butter

1 small carrot, diced

1 small red potato, diced

2 tablespoons peas

1/8 teaspoon thyme, crushed

1/4 teaspoon parsley

1/2 cup milk (regular or soy)

1 cup fish stock or water

1. Melt the butter in a medium saucepan. Once melted, add the water or fish stock.
2. Add peas, carrots, and potatoes to the saucepan.
3. Rinse the fish fillet and remove all bones. Cut into small pieces and add to the saucepan. Cook for 15–20 minutes. The fish should flake easily and the vegetables should be getting tender.
4. Add the milk, thyme, and parsley. Simmer for another 5–10 minutes. Either serve as a chunky soup, or purée in the food processor.

Chowder

Use any mild white fish in this chowder recipe. Clams are typically chewy and not the best to offer a young eater, but an excellent chowder can still be made with fish instead.

Fun Tuna Fishcakes

2 SERVINGS

1 boneless fillet tuna (about 3–4 ounces)	1 egg
1 medium red potato	1 teaspoon parsley
2 cups water or fish stock	1 tablespoon oil
	½ cup bread crumbs

1. Rinse the fillet and remove all bones. Cut into small pieces.
2. Wash, peel, and dice the potato.
3. Bring the water to a boil in a medium saucepan. Add the fish and potato, then cook for 20–25 minutes, or until the fish is cooked and the potato is tender.
4. Fork-mash the fish and potato in a small bowl. Add the egg and parsley, and mix. Form into patties. Roll each patty in bread crumbs.
5. Heat the oil in a non-stick skillet. Sauté the patties 2–3 minutes, or until lightly browned, then flip and repeat. Drain and serve.

Substitution

Fresh out of fresh tuna? Don't despair; these fishcakes can be made just as easily using a boneless fillet of white fish such as orange roughy or sole.

Fish-Potato-Broccoli, Oh My, Pie

🪑 🪑 🪑 🪑 🪑 🪑

6 SERVINGS

1 boneless fillet white fish
2 medium red potatoes, diced
1 medium carrot, diced
½ cup broccoli, diced
1 cup water
½ cup milk (regular or soy)
1 tablespoon all-purpose flour
1 tablespoon butter

1. Rinse the fish fillet and remove all bones. Cut into small pieces.
2. Bring water to a boil in a medium saucepan. Add the potatoes, carrots, and broccoli, then cook for about 10 minutes. Add the fish and cook another 10–15 minutes or until the fish flakes easily. When cooked, drain and return the fish and vegetables to the saucepan.

Adding a Crust

For a more "adult" version of this recipe, try making it using a single-shelled pie crust. A single pie crust consists of mixing 1⅓ cups flour with ½ cup vegetable shortening. When mixed, slowly add 3 tablespoons of ice water. Once a dough is formed, use immediately or store in the refrigerator (wrapped in plastic) until ready for use.

3. In a separate small saucepan, melt the butter. Stir in the flour. Once mixed, add in the milk and stir constantly until a thin sauce is formed. Mix this sauce in with the fish and vegetables, stirring to combine.
4. Divide the fish and vegetables into a 6-cup muffin tin. Bake at 350°F for 30 minutes. Let cool before serving, and fork-mash if desired.

Muffin Pie

Most toddlers have difficulty with hard pie crust, so this "pie" recipe is minus the shell. Baking it in muffin tins provides single-servings and easy leftovers.

Must-Have Haddock in Orange Sauce

2 SERVINGS

1 boneless fillet haddock or other white fish
¼ cup orange juice
½ teaspoon orange zest

1. Preheat the oven to 350°F.
1. Rinse the fish fillet and remove all bones. Place in a greased baking dish.
3. Mix the orange juice and orange zest in a small bowl. Pour over the fish and spread the zest with a fork, making sure the fish gets an even coating.
4. Bake at 350°F for 15–20 minutes. The fish is cooked when it's opaque, and flakes easily with a fork.
5. Spoon the remaining sauce from the pan over the fish, then cut into bite-size pieces before serving.

Orange Zest
Orange zest can be obtained from an orange peel using a zester, but don't despair if you don't have this specialized instrument. You can also rub the orange against a fine grater instead—the peel that comes off will be ground enough for use as zest.

Healthful Carrot and Squash Soup

5 SERVINGS

½ small butternut
squash
6 cups water or veg-
etable stock
⅛ teaspoon oregano,
crushed
⅛ teaspoon thyme,
crushed

1 small clove garlic,
minced
2 medium carrots
½ small onion, diced
1 tablespoon butter or
margarine

1. Peel the squash, remove the seeds and pulp, and cut into chunks.
2. Melt the butter in a large saucepan. Add the onion and garlic, sautéeing until the onion becomes translucent.
3. Add the squash, carrot, and vegetable stock. Bring to a boil, then add oregano and thyme. Reduce to a simmer and cook for 1–2 hours, or until the vegetables are tender. When the soup is done, purée in a food processor or blender before serving.

Why Purée a Soup?

Some soups are meant to be eaten. Minestrone soup, for example, has bites of beans, pasta, and other items that have their own distinct textures. Tomato and squash soup, though, are examples of soups that are best served with a smooth texture. These soups are well-accompanied by toast, crackers, or bread-sticks for dipping.

Veggie Soup to Warm Your Soul

3 SERVINGS

½ cup kidney beans, cooked
½ cup green beans
1 medium red potato, diced
1 medium carrot, diced
½ small onion, diced
1 tablespoon butter or margarine
dash of salt and pepper
4 cups chicken stock or water

1. Snap the ends off the green beans, then cut into 1-inch segments.
2. Melt the butter in a large saucepan. Add the onion, then sauté until it becomes translucent.
3. Add potato, carrot, green beans, kidney beans, salt, pepper, and chicken stock. Bring to a boil, then simmer for at least 1 hour. Longer cooking will make the vegetables more tender and enhance the flavors, but 1 hour is the minimum cooking time.
4. If desired, fork-mash the vegetables before serving.

Vegetable Soup

Vegetable soup is one of the most flexible recipes out there. Use chicken, vegetable, or beef stock for added flavor—black beans or chickpeas instead of kidney beans are acceptable substitutes as well. Clean out your vegetable drawer while creating several healthy meals for your toddler!

Gentle Lentil Stew

1 SERVING

½ cup lentils
2 cups water
¼ teaspoon garlic powder
½ celery stalk, diced
1 plum tomato, diced

1. Bring water to a boil. Add the lentils, tomato, celery, and garlic.
2. Simmer for 2 ½–3 hours.

Easy Lentils

Lentil stew is a healthy meal that requires little attention on the part of the chef. Once it's simmering, you can leave it alone for 2–3 hours.

Chicken Stew with Dumplings

4 SERVINGS

1 drumstick or thigh piece of chicken
6 cups of water
1 medium carrot, diced
1 small Russet potato, diced
1 cup chicken broth
dash of salt and pepper
⅛ teaspoon dill
1 cup all-purpose flour
1 egg
¼ cup water

1. Wash the chicken well, and remove the skin if desired. Bring to a boil in water. Simmer for 1–1½ hours, or until the meat begins falling off the bone.
2. Remove the meat from the pot. Take off all the fat, skin, and bones. Shred the chicken into small pieces, then add back to the pot.

Creamier Stew

If your family prefers their stews on the creamy side (and no one has an intolerance or allergy to dairy products), you can add a can of commercial cream of mushroom or cream of celery soup instead of the broth to the stew during the last hour of simmering. In terms of just thickening the stew, adding dumplings should do the job.

3. Add potatoes and carrots to the chicken pot, along with the salt, pepper, and dill. Simmer for 30–40 minutes, or until the vegetables are tender.
4. Lightly beat the egg, then add in the flour. Stir well, then add water 1 tablespoon at a time until a stiff dough is formed. Roll out the dough, then cut into small strips.
5. Bring the chicken pot back to a boil. Add in the dumplings, then simmer for an additional 40–45 minutes.

Chicken Stew

Chicken stew is not a particularly fast recipe, but it's one that doesn't require constant attention. The boiling and simmering stages can all go longer than recommended; it will soften the veggies and increase the flavors.

A Mean Bean Stew

1 SERVING

½ cup white beans, cooked
¼ pound ground pork sausage
1 medium carrot, diced
dash of paprika
dash of salt
dash of pepper
dash of oregano, crushed

1. Cook the sausage in a medium saucepan, browning until it's completely cooked.
2. Drain the fat from the sausage, then add 2 cups of water and bring to a boil. Add the beans, carrot and spices.
3. Simmer for 1 ½–2 hours.

Hot Variation

If your child has a penchant for spice, try using spicy sausage instead of its more benign cousin. For other family members who like their food spicier, you can add a little Tabasco to their bowl before serving. Don't assume that your toddler won't like spicy food—many toddlers actually prefer highly flavored foods by this age.

Classic Turkey Noodle Soup

4 SERVINGS

1 leftover turkey carcass
1 cup dried egg noodles
1 medium Russet
   potato, diced
1 medium carrot, diced

1 stalk celery, diced
½ medium onion, diced
1 teaspoon salt
1 teaspoon pepper

1. Place the leftover turkey carcass, along with the salt and pepper, in a large saucepan and cover with water. Bring to a boil, then simmer for about 3 hours.
2. Strain the turkey stock. Tear the leftover turkey into shreds, discarding the fat and bones. Put 4 cups of stock in a medium saucepan.
3. Add potato, carrot, celery, and onion to the turkey stock. Bring to a boil, then reduce to a simmer. Simmer for 1 hour.
4. Add in the egg noodles and turkey meat, then simmer for another 45 minutes.

Post-Thanksgiving Leftovers

This classic recipe is good after Thanksgiving (it makes excellent use of the leftover turkey) but can be made just as easily by using chicken stock instead.

Summer Macaroni Salad

1 SERVING

½ cup cooked macaroni
1 tablespoon mayonnaise
½ small pickle
dash of pepper
dash of onion powder

1. Dice the pickle into very small pieces, then mix with the macaroni.
2. Mix in the mayonnaise.
3. Toss with the onion powder and pepper.

Make Your Own Macaroni Salad

Don't eat the warmed-over picnic macaroni salad—make your own from scratch! Use leftover cooked macaroni to speed up the preparation time.

Cauliflower with Cheese Please

1 SERVING

½ cup cauliflower
2 cups water
2 ounces cheese

1. Wash the cauliflower, dice into small florets, and place in a steamer basket. Fill the bottom of a saucepan with water, place the steamer basket inside, then bring to a boil. Cook for 15 minutes, or until the cauliflower is tender.
2. Melt the cheese in a microwave-safe bowl. Heat in the microwave in 30-second intervals, stirring in between, until well-melted.
3. Place the cooked cauliflower in a bowl and pour the melted cheese on top.

Glorious Leftovers

Spicing up leftovers is a great way to serve a fresh new meal in no time at all. Use whatever ingredients are on hand—mild spices, melted cheese, diced ham—to turn any meal into something new and delightful. It's easier and more convenient than cooking a whole new meal from scratch every night, and you may stumble on some amazing combinations.

Dynamic Duo: Pasta and Broccoli

2 SERVINGS

1 cup pasta
½ cup broccoli
½ clove garlic, minced
4 cups water

1 teaspoon olive oil
1 teaspoon grated
   Parmesan
1 teaspoon parsley

1. Wash the broccoli and dice into small florets.
2. Bring the water to a boil. Add the pasta, then cook for about 10 minutes. Add in the broccoli and cook for another 10 minutes, or until both pasta and broccoli are tender. When cooked, drain.
3. Heat the olive oil in a medium skillet. Add garlic and parsley, sautéing for 2–3 minutes.
4. Add the pasta and broccoli to the saucepan. Sauté for 2–3 minutes, tossing the pasta and broccoli together with the garlic.
5. Sprinkle with Parmesan cheese before serving.

Garlic

Go as easy (or as heavy) on the garlic as your toddler seems to like. You can easily use part of a clove, or an entire clove if she seems to like it. This is also a perfect dish for serving to the rest of the family, and it won't require any additional seasonings.

Peanut Buttery Noodles

2 SERVINGS

½ cup spaghetti
2 cups water
¼ cup chicken or vegetable stock
1 tablespoon peanut butter
1 tablespoon soy sauce
½ teaspoon ginger, minced

1. Bring the water to a boil. Add the spaghetti and cook for 15 minutes, or until the pasta is tender. Drain the noodles when they're cooked.
2. In a small saucepan, mix the stock, peanut butter, soy sauce, and ginger. Heat until peanut butter is just melted, stirring well.
3. Toss the noodles with the sauce.
4. For older children, serve with a small handful of chopped peanuts.

Origins of Soy Sauce

When soy sauce is made in the traditional way, soybeans are mixed with roasted wheat or rice and then fermented. After this process is complete (and it can take 2–3 months), the beans are drained and strained. The resulting liquid is soy sauce. Soybeans are an amazingly versatile legume!

Fluffy Lemon Pudding

4 SERVINGS

1 egg, separated
½ cup sugar
2 tablespoons all-
purpose flour

3 tablespoons lemon
juice
2 teaspoons lemon zest
½ cup milk (regular/soy)
dash salt

1. Preheat oven to 350°F.
2. Place the egg yolk in a bowl. Beat in sugar. Add in the flour, salt, and lemon zest. Stir in lemon juice and milk, and mix well.
3. In a separate bowl, whip the egg white to soft peaks using an electric mixer. Beat on high until when you lift one of the beaters out of the bowl, the egg whites form small white peaks. Fold the egg white into the rest of the batter.
4. Pour into a baking dish. Bake for 45 minutes.
5. Let cool before serving, though adults may prefer the pudding warm. Store leftovers in the refrigerator.

Safety First

There are recipes for lemon pudding that don't involve baking, but most of them involve raw eggs. Try this one—it's a bit more work, but much safer for your toddler.

Best Banana Pudding

2 SERVINGS

1 ripe banana
⅓ cup sugar
¾ cup milk (regular or soy)
1 egg
2 teaspoons cornstarch
¼ teaspoon vanilla extract

1. Whisk the egg in a small bowl. Beat in sugar.
2. Stir in the milk and cornstarch, mixing thoroughly.
3. Fork-mash the banana until it is completely creamed.
4. Pour the pudding mixture and banana into a small saucepan. Bring to a boil, then reduce the heat to medium. Stirring constantly, cook for 4–5 minutes, or until the pudding thickens.
5. Turn off the heat and stir in the vanilla. Mix well, then allow to cool before serving.

Layer It Up

A traditional way to serve banana pudding is a layered presentation in a glass or plastic bowl. Start with a layer of pudding, then follow with a layer of crushed vanilla wafer cookies. Add a layer of thinly sliced bananas, then another layer of pudding. Top it off with a dollop of whipped cream.

Lemony Rice Pudding

4 SERVINGS

½ cup rice
1 cup water
2 tablespoons milk or
    cream
1 teaspoon butter or
    margarine

1 egg
2 tablespoons brown
    sugar
1 tablespoon lemon juice
½ teaspoon lemon zest

1. Bring the water, rice, and butter to a boil in a medium saucepan.
2. Reduce heat to a simmer, then stir in the cream. Once the rice returns to a simmer, cook for 25–30 minutes, or until the liquid is absorbed.
3. Turn down the heat to very low. Beat the egg and stir it into the rice pot.
4. Add in the lemon juice, lemon zest, and sugar. Mix thoroughly and continue to stir until the pudding thickens.
5. Remove from heat, and allow to cool before serving. Refrigerate the leftovers immediately.

Lemon Pudding

This pudding is not as creamy as some; rather, it offers a soft texture from the rice, mixed with the sweet-sour sensation of sugar and lemons.

Cool Vanilla Custard

1 SERVING

1 egg
2 tablespoons sugar
1 tablespoon cornstarch
½ cup milk (regular or soy)
¼ teaspoon vanilla extract

1. In a small bowl, whisk the egg together with the sugar. When mixed, stir in the cornstarch.
2. Add in vanilla and milk, stirring until they are completely combined.
3. Pour the mixture into a medium saucepan. Heat to scalding, reduce the heat to medium, and stir until the mixture thickens. Keep stirring, or the cornstarch is likely to become lumpy.
4. Once thick, pour the custard into a pan or small glass dish and cover it with plastic wrap. Refrigerate for several hours before serving.

Plan Ahead

Vanilla custard is a soothing dish that is best served cold, so don't start this recipe 5 minutes before you plan to eat it! Refrigerate it for 2–3 hours before serving.

Best Chocolate Banana Custard

I SERVING

¼ cup semisweet chocolate chips
1 teaspoon butter
1 ripe banana
1 egg
2 tablespoons sugar
1 tablespoon cornstarch
½ cup milk (regular or soy)
¼ teaspoon vanilla extract

1. Put the chocolate and butter into a microwave-safe dish. Microwave on low, in 30-second intervals, until the chocolate is melted. Stir well after each interval to see if the chocolate is sufficiently melted.
2. Fork-mash the banana until it is completely creamed.
3. In a small bowl, whisk the egg together with the sugar. When mixed, stir in the cornstarch.

Frozen Bananas

Chocolate and bananas make a fantastic combination, so this custard should come as no surprise! If you find yourself with leftover melted chocolate, try coating a banana with it and freezing for a couple hours—frozen bananas will win you some bonus points with the kids.

4. Add vanilla and milk, stirring until they are completely combined. Pour in the melted chocolate and banana, stirring to combine.
5. Pour the mixture into a medium saucepan. Heat to scalding, reduce the heat to medium, and stir until the mixture thickens. Keep stirring, or the cornstarch is likely to become lumpy.
6. Once thick, pour the custard into a small heatproof glass dish and cover it with plastic wrap. Refrigerate for several hours before serving.

Vanilla Beans

If you like your spices right from the source, try using vanilla beans instead of vanilla extract. Vanilla beans may be difficult to find in regular grocery stores, but they're inexpensive and highly flavorful. Replace a teaspoon of vanilla extract with about 1 inch of bean. Just make sure to remove the bean before serving!

Coconut Egg Custard Creation

1 SERVING

1 egg
2 tablespoons sugar
1 tablespoon
    cornstarch

¼ teaspoon vanilla
    extract
½ cup coconut milk
¼ cup milk (regular/soy)
¼ cup shredded coconut

1. In a small bowl, whisk the egg together with the sugar. When mixed, stir in the cornstarch.
2. Add in the vanilla, coconut milk, and milk, stirring until they are completely combined. Stir in shredded coconut.
3. Pour the mixture into a medium saucepan. Heat to scalding, reduce the heat to medium, and stir until the mixture thickens. Keep stirring, or the cornstarch is likely to become lumpy.
4. Once thick, pour the custard into a small heat-proof glass dish and cover it with plastic wrap. Refrigerate for several hours before serving.

A Sweeter Touch

You can sweeten up any custard recipe by substituting half the milk with sweetened condensed milk. Because there's no soy-based version of condensed milk, you won't be able to make a non-dairy version.

Strawberry Icy Pops

4 SERVINGS

1 ½ cups water
½ cup orange juice
4 large strawberries

1. Purée the strawberries in a food processor or blender.
2. Add water and orange juice to the food processor and mix until completely combined.
3. Pour into a rack of 4 ice pop molds. Freeze for at least 5 hours before serving.

Make Your Own Molds

If you don't have plastic molds, try using disposable paper cups to make this summertime treat. Insert a popsicle stick once partially frozen, then simply peel off the cup when it's time to eat.

Homemade Vanilla Ice Cream

2 SERVINGS

¾ cup milk
¼ cup sugar
2 egg yolks
1 cup cream

½ teaspoon vanilla
   extract
8–10 cups of ice cubes
1–2 cups rock salt

1. Heat the milk to scalding. Add in sugar, reduce the heat to medium and stir until the sugar is dissolved. Add in egg yolks and stir for 1 minute.
2. Remove from heat when it begins to thicken into custard. Add cream and vanilla. Stir.
3. Pour into a small plastic container. Place this container inside a larger bowl. Fill the bowl with ice and salt so that your ice-cream container is surrounded on all sides.
4. Stir the ice cream constantly for about 15-20 minutes. When the ice cream starts feeling cold and thick, it's getting close to being done. You can also pour the custard mix into a sealing plastic baggie, then knead it inside the ice and salt.

Ice Cream

While ice cream is easy to make in an ice-cream maker, it's possible to do it yourself without any specialized equipment. Be prepared for a workout, though! You may need to enlist a friend with strong arm muscles.

Fantastic Frozen Fruit

1 SERVING

4 grapes
1 strawberry
½ banana

1. Wash the grapes and slice in half. Wash the strawberry, remove the hull, and slice into quarters. Peel the banana and slice into coins.
2. Place the fruit in a disposable paper cup.
3. Freeze for at least 4 hours before serving.

Party Tips

Frozen fruit is great for a summer birthday party. To make this simple dessert a little more festive, freeze the fruit in printed paper muffin cups or in decorated snack-sized zipper baggies. For added color, try using both red and green grapes, pineapple, and maraschino cherries. You can even add some watermelon, cantaloupe, or honeydew to produce a rainbow effect.

Peanut Butter Goodies

8 SERVINGS

½ cup crushed
   graham crackers
3 ounces semisweet
   chocolate

1 tablespoon shortening
1 cup powdered sugar
½ cup peanut butter
¼ cup chocolate chips

1. Place the graham crackers in a sealing plastic bag. Crush with your hands or a mallet to make coarse crumbs (this is a great task for toddlers.)
2. Put the chocolate and shortening into a microwave-safe dish. Microwave on low, in 30-second intervals, until the chocolate is melted. Stir well after each microwave interval.
3. Mix the chocolate and sugar together until they're combined. Stir in peanut butter.
4. Add graham cracker crumbs. Mix gently until they are completely incorporated. Add chocolate chips and stir until thoroughly mixed.
5. Press into a loaf pan; cut into cookies about 1" x 2".

Making Parents Feel Better

If the thought of gooey treats makes you want to run for the toothpaste, you can mitigate the health concerns by adding a tablespoon of wheat germ to these peanut butter goodies. Also, instead of chocolate chips, try throwing in a few "twigs" of an oat bran cereal.

Blueberry Crumble

2 SERVINGS

1 cup blueberries
2 teaspoons white sugar
1 teaspoon brown sugar
1 tablespoon butter
¼ cup oatmeal

1. Preheat the oven to 350°F. Wash the blueberries. Place into a small baking dish. Mix the white sugar into the berries.
2. In a separate small dish, mash the butter, brown sugar, and oatmeal together with a fork.
3. When the mixture forms small crumbs, sprinkle over the top of the berries.
4. Bake for 30 minutes, or until the topping is brown and crunchy. Cool to room temperature before serving.

Toppings

Fruit crumbles are simple desserts that go well with Homemade Ice Cream or whipped cream. It also goes nicely with Custard Topping.

Love That Sponge Cake

🪑 🪑 🪑 🪑 🪑 🪑 🪑 🪑

8 SERVINGS

3 *eggs*
1 *cup all-purpose flour*
⅔ *cup sugar*
2 *tablespoons melted butter or margarine*

1. Preheat the oven to 375°F.
2. Beat the eggs and sugar together in a medium bowl; mix until the eggs have a light, fluffy consistency. Add in the melted butter, stirring until it's thoroughly combined.
3. Mix in flour, and pour the batter into a greased 8-inch cake pan.
4. Bake for about 20–25 minutes, or until a toothpick inserted into the middle of the cake comes out clean. The cake should have a slightly springy consistency when the top is lightly pressed.

Quick Serve

Here's a sweet treat for your toddler that is made from only four ingredients. It's quick to prepare and flavored simply enough to appeal to most children.

Peachy Grape Gelatin

6 SERVINGS

1 small package (3 ounces) peach-flavored gelatin
   mix
½ cup grapes
½ ripe peach
2 cups water

1. Wash the peach, then remove the skin and pit. Dice into small pieces.
2. Wash the grapes and slice in half.
3. Bring 1 cup of water to a boil in a medium saucepan. Stir in gelatin mix and cook until completely dissolved.
4. Remove from heat. Stir in 1 cup of cold water and the diced fruit.
5. Pour into a lightly greased gelatin mold or dish. Refrigerate until set, 3–4 hours.

Quick Set

Don't want to wait several hours for your gelatin dessert? Try cooking it using the "quick set" method. Boil ½ cup of water to mix into the gelatin. Once dissolved, add in ½ cup of cold water and 1 cup ice cubes. With this method, you'll only need to refrigerate it for 1 hour or less.

Perfect Fruit Parfait

2 SERVINGS

½ cup heavy whipping cream

3 ounces cream cheese

¼ cup sugar

½ cup strawberries

¼ cup blueberries

¼ cup peaches

¼ cup honeydew or cantaloupe

¼ cup grapes

1. Wash all the fruit. Remove any stems or seeds, then dice into small pieces.
2. Whip the whipping cream using an electric mixer. Alternatively, use 1 cup of pre-whipped regular or non-dairy topping.
3. Mix the cream cheese and sugar together in a small bowl. Gently stir in the whipped cream.
4. In a transparent plastic cup, place a 1-inch layer of fruit. Follow with a 1-inch layer of cream cheese. Repeat until fruit and cheese are used. This recipe should make 2 medium cups.

Creamy Parfait

Prepare a packet of berry-flavored gelatin according to the package directions. After it has solidified in the refrigerator, mix it with an equal amount whipped cream. Use this cream as an alternating layer with fruit, and presto! Parfait magic.

Index

Help Is on the Way from Adams Media!

(Spiral-bound trade paperback, $12.95)

ISBN 10: 1-59869-332-8
ISBN 13: 978-1-59869-332-4

ISBN 10: 1-59869-333-6
ISBN 13: 978-1-59869-333-1

ISBN 10: 1-59869-334-4
ISBN 13: 978-1-59869-334-8

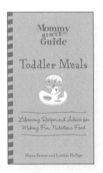

ISBN 10: 1-59869-331-X
ISBN 13: 978-1-59869-331-7

Available wherever books are sold.

Or call us at 1-800-258-0929 or visit us at www.adamsmedia.com.